# Soft Skills for Children

# Soft Skills for Children

*A Guide for Parents and Teachers*

Nancy Armstrong Melser

ROWMAN & LITTLEFIELD
Lanham • Boulder • New York • London

Published by Rowman & Littlefield
An imprint of The Rowman & Littlefield Publishing Group, Inc.
4501 Forbes Boulevard, Suite 200, Lanham, Maryland 20706
www.rowman.com

6 Tinworth Street, London SE11 5AL

British Library Cataloguing in Publication Information Available

**Library of Congress Cataloging-in-Publication Data**

ISBN 9781475851762 (cloth : alk. paper)
ISBN 9781475851779 (pbk. : alk. paper)
ISBN 9781475851786 (electronic)

∞ ™ The paper used in this publication meets the minimum requirements of American National Standard for Information Sciences Permanence of Paper for Printed Library Materials, ANSI/NISO Z39.48-1992.

# Contents

# Preface

Soft skills is a catchphrase in the world of business. Numerous websites and books exist on the topic of soft skills as they apply to career searches and job preparedness. Employers are looking for well-rounded applicants who know the *hard skills* or background information and technical skills that are necessary for jobs. However, they are also looking for employees who have *soft skills* as well.

According to Dictionary.com (2018), soft skills are defined as "personal attributes that enable someone to interact effectively and harmoniously with other people." As a teacher and educator for more than 25 years, I have noticed that while the majority of my pre-service teachers were wonderful and well-prepared, there were always a handful of students who were lacking soft skills in the field of teaching. These future teachers would sometimes lack confidence, professionalism, and good work ethic.

After working with future teachers who were lacking in professional and people skills, I decided to give a survey to school superintendents and administrators about what was lacking in today's pre-service teachers. One respondent simply stated, "Soft skills." Curious about this answer, I began researching soft skills as they applied to teachers. I completed presentations and wrote my first book, entitled *Teaching Soft Skills in a Hard World: Skills for Beginning Teachers.*

A week after submitting my book for publication, I received an email from a state legislator announcing a new requirement for K–12 students for employment and future job skills (Indiana Senate Bill 297, 2018). In the email, the term soft skills was mentioned once again, but this time, soft skills were being applied to help children become college and career ready. As a teacher and parent, I was immediately interested in this idea as it applied to school-age students and wanted to embark on another book that applied to such a demographic group.

I researched the term soft skills and found that it applied mostly to the business world, not to children. However, if we expect our K-12 students to be prepared for future jobs and become enabled with the skills necessary to be successful, why not start with young children and focus on these skills throughout their entire school preparation?

This book focuses on fourteen soft skills that are important for children to learn. While some of the skills such as communication skills and time management overlap with the book, I wrote for beginning teachers; others are aimed more at a younger population of students. The ideas for this book come from my experience as a parent, teacher, and teacher educator and are based on events that I encountered with my son and my students—both at the elementary and university level.

As a teacher, I know that soft skills are also used in the classroom. When teachers model appropriate behaviors, show students how to respond appropriately, and use strategies that incorporate the skills needed for tomorrow's careers, they are teaching soft skills that children will use for their future. The sections I included in this book for educators outline ways to incorporate soft skills into classrooms as well.

As a parent, I learned about soft skills by watching my son interact with other children on the playground, through sports teams, and around my kitchen table. Now that he is a teenager and nearing his own entrance to college and then a future career, I realize that soft skills were an important part of his upbringing—though I did not use the title of soft skills at the time. Much of what I write in this book are commonsense parenting skills that most parents do as second nature. However, having them in print will allow parents to focus on these skills in an intentional way.

I would like to offer two sidenotes about the information presented in this book. First, while I address *parents* in each chapter, I realize that this goes beyond just birth parents and includes family members, stepparents, grandparents, and, honestly, anyone who is an adult figure in the lives of children. I believe that anyone willing to help a child become a more competent, well-rounded individual is welcome to participate!

I also use the words *kids* and *children* throughout the book. In my house, anyone that is living under my roof is considered a child, from birth until they obtain jobs and are not living in my basement! Kids is simply a word that is understood by readers and one with which both parents and teachers can identify with.

By working in collaboration, both teachers and parents can concentrate their efforts on the soft skills that are needed for tomorrow's jobs. Using soft skills will educate children about the ways to get along with others, have self-skills that will help them be productive in life, and learn strategies for successful careers in the future. By learning soft skills as children, they will be able to make the world a better place—one skill at a time.

# Acknowledgments

I want to acknowledge and dedicate this book to my son, Tyler. He has taught me many things about life and has tolerated having a teacher-mom as a parent. As I wrote the chapter on resiliency, I realized just how much he has been through in his 18 short years and how he always comes back with a smile. It shows me that, along with his dad, he has been taught the soft skills presented in this book—often without knowing it! I wish that the teachers who read this book will have many Tylers in their classrooms. I hope that the parents who read it can have the pleasure of raising such a great child, and I wish them well on this journey we call parenthood.

# Introduction

Children today are growing up in a world of uncertainty. The ever-changing political climate, fear of mass shootings in their own schools, and issues such as cyberbullying are taking over their once *safe havens.*

Children are identified more and more as *traumatized, fragile,* and *unreachable.* They have more on their plates than in the past and are in need of some answers to help them see a brighter future. Children are growing up faster than ever, and many spend far too much time in front of a screen instead of frolicking outdoors, as young people did in the past.

Teachers and administrators deal with misbehavior, lack of motivation, and social issues in schools and classrooms, constantly struggling with how to meet the needs of all children while teaching an ever-changing curriculum that is required by law. They are leaving the profession of teaching burnt out and seeking a more positive avenue to gear their efforts.

What can be done to help children learn in a more positive environment, feel safe in the classrooms in which they are placed, and feel valued and respected by those with whom they learn? One possible answer is *soft skills.*

According to Dictionary.com (2018), soft skills are defined as "personal attributes that enable someone to interact effectively and harmoniously with other people." Although working with others is an important part of succeeding in today's classrooms, soft skills goes beyond just *getting along.* Soft skills are also the skills that students need to reach future goals, remain optimistic, and deal with conflict in their schooling. Soft skills also prepare them for future problems, be responsible citizens, and obtain jobs that will empower them in the future.

In the adult world, many books and websites exist about soft skills in the workforce. According to Monster.com, a website that focuses on job skills and careers for adults, soft skills are important in obtaining and keeping a job. "Basically, you can be the best at what you do, but if your soft skills aren't cutting it, you're limiting your chances of career success" (Monster.com, August 5, 2018).

If adults are to be prepared and ready for the real world, why not start teaching these skills to children? A recent Senate bill in the State of Indiana requires the teaching of an "employability skills curriculum" (Senate Bill 297). This curriculum requires schools to teach the soft skills needed to be successful in future careers, such as following directions and arriving on time to work. Although these skills may not be used for years to come, why not start teaching them in a K-12 curriculum?

## HARD SKILLS VS. SOFT SKILLS

Soft skills, as outlined above, are the skills that help one get along with others, be prepared for the future of professional behaviors, and have the ability to be flexible and make good decisions. These skills are often hard to measure but are important to the success of one's future career.

Hard skills, on the other hand, are the skills that one learns in a school curriculum. These include the measurable items that are found in a curriculum map or scope and sequence, such as being able to comprehend what one reads, have computation skills for math, and knowing about skills, such as how the government operates and how to make good decisions for one's health and wellness. They are taught, tested, and evaluated on a daily basis, and students receive homework to practice these skills.

Hard skills are also the focus of standardized tests and are measured to determine one's success in school and admission to college. Hard skills receive letter grades and impact grade point averages in the lives of students. However, simply knowing the material and passing tests is not enough in today's world.

Being able to communicate with others, be responsible, and work as part of a team are all important characteristics for succeeding in the future as well. Also, being able to have a positive attitude, show composure, and be motivated to do one's best are also vital to accomplishing one's goals. The soft skills of being able to work with others and maintain composure go hand in hand with the hard skills of having the knowledge and ability to do the job well.

As employers look for future job applicants, they need to know who has the hard skills to do the job but also have the soft skills as well. Knowing that an individual has both sets of skills means that a person is well-rounded both in information but in disposition as well. This book will examine strategies that can be used by both parents and educators to teach the soft skills that are needed to meet the demands of today's world.

Through collaboration from families and schools, children can learn the soft skills needed for their future at an early age and with activities that are probably already happening at home and in classrooms. Though there are probably hundreds of soft skills that are needed for a well-rounded child, this book will focus on fourteen of the most important soft skills for children. Each soft skill has an explanation of the components of the skill as well as how teachers and parents can teach each skill in the context of experiences and events that are happening in the lives of children.

## HOW EDUCATORS CAN TEACH SOFT SKILLS

Teachers are an important component of teaching soft skills to children. Since students spend a great deal of time in classrooms, knowing that they have a caring teacher who will provide guidance, influence choices, and teach strategies for success are all key to creating well-rounded individuals.

Educators are key to teaching soft skills since they teach a curriculum that encompasses the skills needed for the jobs of tomorrow. They teach hard skills, which include content and technical skills, but they also teach the social skills that will be needed to work with others and be productive citizens in the future.

Modeling by teachers is also vital to developing soft skills in children. Since children are always watching the reaction of their teachers, the way they handle stress in the classroom, and how they manage time and organization, students will likely model the behaviors of their teachers in these areas as well. Having teachers who model the soft skills presented in this book will enable children to enter the workforce prepared and ready for the problems and opportunities they will encounter.

Finally, collaboration with parents will help children see that there is a team of caring adults who want to help students make good decisions, learn empathy and respect for others, and have positive outlooks toward their future. By working together with families, teachers can make a huge impact on the future success of children in their classrooms. They can prepare students for the challenges of tomorrow and empower them to be the best they can be. By working together to teach soft skills, the world will be a better place for children.

## HOW PARENTS CAN TEACH SOFT SKILLS

Parents are a child's first teachers. They are there from the first day of a child's life to teach and model the appropriate behaviors. They share experiences, offer advice, and help children to make good decisions and learn from their bad choices. Parents provide guidance for their families and help them grow and develop into well-rounded individuals.

Families are important in the development of soft skills such as teaching good manners and organization skills. By developing these skills at a young age, parents will be able to help mold children who are respectful and kind to others. They will also show children that soft skills are key to having a successful school experience and, in their futures, as they enter the real world of work and careers.

Parents also model the soft skills contained in this book, whether purposefully or not. Children are always watching their parents to see how they handle difficult situations, make decisions, and handle themselves when things do not go as planned. Children are like sponges, and they absorb the characteristics of their parents and the way that the parents deal with uncertainty and face life's struggles. Knowing that children are modeling a parent's behavior can impact the way that parents react to situations and problems they may encounter.

Finally, collaboration between the school and teacher with parents will enable children to see a partnership of caring adults who want students to be successful in life. By learning about soft skills both in classrooms and at home, children can see that the soft skills in this book are important in all areas of a child's world.

# ONE

## Communication Skills

- Why are communication skills important to children?
- How can educators teach communication skills to children?
- How can parents teach communication skills to children?

### IMPORTANCE OF COMMUNICATION SKILLS

Communication skills include being able to effectively speak, listen, read, and write. Communicating means sharing ideas with others, responding respectfully to the ideas of those around us, and being able to correspond with people with whom we work and play. Communication skills start after the birth of a child. When children hear a mother's voice or a father making noises with a toy, they realize that sound represents something.

The first part of communication involves speaking to others. It implies that children have a basic set of oral language skills that enable them to talk and communicate. However, it can also include sign language, braille, and other methods of adaptive communication. Regardless of the method one uses, it implies that people share both words and ideas. Learning to communicate with others is a skill that begins very early in life.

Communication also involves listening skills. Being able to be an effective listener means that one has the skills of eye contact, active listening, and the ability to paraphrase and comprehend what the speaker says. Teaching children to be good listeners implies that the child can interact with others but also pay attention to information that is being given.

Body language is also included in communication skills for children. According to Dr. Albert Mehrabian (1980), a researcher on nonverbal communication, only 7 percent of a message is sent through words, 38 percent through vocal features, and 55 percent through nonverbal communication such as facial expressions and body language.

Teaching a child that one's facial expressions and body language can impact communication is also an important skill to teach. If a child says that he has done his homework but has a smirk on his face, parents and teachers will quickly pick up on the body language and know that something is out of place. Body language can also tell friends, families, and others how confident a child is feeling or how nervous one is. Teaching how to overcome some of these feelings can help a child with this skill far into the future.

Communication also includes the use of technology. Learning proper phone etiquette, email manners, and texting protocols will be useful to children. As technology use increases across the world, being able to use a cell phone properly, send an appropriate email to a teacher, or a text to a friend are all skills that parents and teachers can teach and refine as children begin using these technologies. Also, teaching children about the impact of cyberbullying and appropriate website usage are important skills for children to learn as well.

Overall, making sure that children know how to speak and listen effectively are key ingredients in raising a well-rounded child who is ready for the future. Making sure that children can communicate respectfully, look a person in the eye, and use a confident voice will be helpful for school presentations, social activities, and even interviews for college or jobs. The soft skill of communication can be taught and modeled by both teachers and parents and is indeed worthy of the time and energy it takes to teach.

The next section will explain ways that educators can teach communication skills to their children. From teaching the basic curriculum involved in language arts to modeling this skill in the classroom, instructors play a vital part in teaching this skill to children.

# HOW CAN EDUCATORS TEACH COMMUNICATION SKILLS?

By the time children arrive in school, much of their language skills have already been formed. However, the communication skills that children need to be successful in life can still be modeled and refined in the classroom. At a very early age, teachers can show children how to effectively speak to their friends, use negotiation skills, and solve problems with their peers.

Teaching children to *use their words* by asking nicely for a toy, sharing with classmates, and solving problems that happen at recess are great ways to teach a child to stand up for themselves or handle a problem that happens with peers. Children need to learn how to compromise and explain how the actions for others can impact them as well. Teaching phrases such as, "When someone takes my toy, I feel sad, and I would like to have it back" puts the words in children's terms and teaches them that communication can be a useful tool when done nicely.

Helping children to feel comfortable speaking to others in the class is also a skill that teachers of young children can do in the classroom. Allowing children to share thoughts and ideas during community circle or show-and-tell encourages them to speak in front of others and shows that they have a voice in the classroom. Many teachers also feel that class meetings in the morning help with classroom management and setting a positive tone for the day.

Teaching children about appropriate volume levels is a great way to teach about communication skills in the classroom as well. Some teachers use the idea of an indoor and outdoor voice when teaching this skill, with the idea that an indoor or quieter voice is used in the classroom so that they do not disturb others, and an outdoor voice is used in physical education classes or on the playground where noisy environments are allowed and expected. By teaching about volume levels, educators are preparing children for the etiquette used in an office setting or even a quiet setting such as a church or place of worship.

Reading is another important part of learning communication skills. Teachers must teach the required elements of reading, such as phonics, word recognition, and decoding, but they also need to teach students to read for information, how to tell if data are from a relevant source, and how to use and interpret what they have read.

Students also need to learn that reading is used for a variety of reasons, including using a recipe for cooking, locating facts for an assignment, or simply reading for pleasure. Making sure that real-life applications are taught and used with children can be a great way to make reading meaningful to students.

The skill of listening is another part of communication that teachers can use in the classroom. Doing activities such as reading out loud and having the children recall information, having students listen to directions and perform an activity accordingly, or doing *talk and turns* with a friend or classmate are all ways to teach children the skill of listening. Many activities are available both commercially and on the Internet that focus on listening skills for children. These activities should be intentionally taught to children to further develop listening skills in the classroom.

Writing is a communication skill as well. Teachers can focus on writing and the many purposes of writing that children will need for the future. The simple skill of relating information, such as creating a grocery list or writing a note to a grandparent, is useful and necessary in today's world. Children who can learn the skill of writing at an early age can realize that this is a powerful tool for communicating and sharing their ideas with others.

Learning to write precise directions for how to do something or communicate through homework activities can also help teach written communication. A wide variety of activities and ways to practice written communication are available to teachers through school curriculum and on the Internet. When taught with a real-life application, students will benefit from these skills and be able to use them in their future.

Writing for personal reasons is also a focus of written communication. Whether it is teaching the children to be reflective and consider another person's point of view or document one's activities through a personal diary, learning to write about one's needs and interests may also be used in the classroom. By using personal reflection, teachers can also get to know the interests of the children in the classroom—a bonus for connecting with one's students.

In brief, there are many ways that teachers can instruct students in the area of communication skills. Although speaking and listening will likely be used the most in social settings and future job assignments, knowing how to use reading and writing in the real world are also important. By working together with parents, teaching children the soft skill of communication is a must to be successful in today's world. The next section will explain the ways that parents can become involved in this process.

## HOW CAN PARENTS TEACH COMMUNICATION SKILLS?

Parents are a child's first teacher and usually the primary caregiver. Therefore, communication starts from the first day of a child's life. When a baby cries to send the message that she is hungry, needs to have a diaper changed, or is tired, parents learn to interpret and respond to a child's needs. While crying is a very basic communication skill, infants learn at a very young age that this simple action gets attention!

When infants and toddlers begin to develop verbal abilities, parents can help refine and teach these skills with their children. Parents can help identify and teach new words as children are curious and find important things around them. As a child points to a flower at the park, parents can explain and teach the word "flower" in context.

Aside from basic language skills, parents can help children to learn the skills of communication as well. Learning to say "thank you" for a gift, "excuse me" when walking in front of others, and a friendly hand-shake when being introduced to a new person are all skills that parents need to teach and explain to children. Teaching children these skills rather than assuming that they will be taught in school is a huge role that parents can do at home. According to Arora (2018):

> Possessing a set of proper oral language skills can be described as an essential life skill in today's times. Parents should start teaching their kids basic communication skills during the early years and go on to hone their skills as they grow. Assuming that kids may learn suitable communication skills sans parental guidance can be a huge mistake. Parents may wish to coach their kids not only to communicate effectively but also politely.

While the skill of using manners is explained in-depth in a future chapter, knowing how to communicate kindly and professionally are skills that will be needed in both the school and future work settings. Another skill involved in communication is the use of social cues.

Social cues are noticing and using the appropriate communication skills in the appropriate setting. Parents can teach social cues in several ways. First, parents can teach that certain settings require certain behaviors. For example, a loud voice is used at the park or when playing with ones' siblings, while a quiet voice is used at a wedding or funeral. Social cues can also include knowing a child's audience. Talking and being silly with friends may not be the same as speaking to older adults or grandparents.

Looking people in the eye while speaking, and standing an appropriate distance from others when talking, are also social cues that can be taught and modeled to children.

Also, social cues such as how to communicate with someone with disabilities or knowing to use a louder voice when speaking to Grandpa are all social situations that children may need to learn, depending on the circumstances.

Overall, learning to communicate effectively is an important soft skill that all children need. From the very beginning stages of infancy, children learn that communicating through crying gets their needs met. However, as they grow and mature, children need to learn that communication is also a way to interact with others and effectively form relationships in both social and professional settings. By teaching the skill of communication at home, parents can model this skill and prepare them for future encounters with others.

## KEY IDEAS

- Communication involves the areas of speaking, listening, reading, and writing.
- While parents may teach beginning verbal skills to children, teachers can refine these skills in the classroom.
- Communication skills are needed to participate in school and social activities effectively, but they also are needed in the workplace.
- Teaching children about body language and social cues can also be helpful in the area of communication.
- Communication through technology also needs to be taught and modeled to children both at home and school.
- Teaching children communication skills through real-life experiences is important so that children learn how this authentically impacts them.

# TWO

## Teamwork

- Why is teamwork an important skill to teach children?
- How can educators teach teamwork to children?
- How can parents teach teamwork to children?

### IMPORTANCE OF TEAMWORK

Teamwork is an important skill in today's world. People work together on projects, committees, and other endeavors that require collaboration and cooperation. They must learn to communicate, value the opinion of others, and learn to compromise. Teamwork is an important skill in careers of the future and is crucial to teach children at an early age.

By learning to work together, children will develop skills that will last a lifetime. Parents and teachers who teach the skill of teamwork are allowing students to be able to work with others—a vital skill in life. According to Lisa McQuerrey (2018):

> For students to achieve a comprehensive, well-rounded education, integrated teamwork on several fronts is vital. Teamwork is necessary between students, between students and teachers, and among parents and educators. The more teamwork fundamentals exhibited, the more opportunity exists for students to learn the vital skills of compromise and collaboration.

Teaching about teamwork and collaboration is not always easy to accomplish. Sometimes the people on the team or committee are difficult to work with, and it takes a great deal of effort to do this skill. Learning to listen to the views of others and coming to a compromise takes careful words and actions to accomplish without hurting feelings or saying the wrong thing.

Teaching children the skill of teamwork includes areas such as negotiation, sharing, and active listening to be successful. Teamwork is not simply throwing kids in groups but also teaching them *how* to work well with others. In real life, conflict occurs, friends have opinions that are different from ours, and people in the office or neighborhood may not always work well together. Children need to learn that working with others is not always easy but that through the skill of teamwork, tasks can be accomplished and work can be completed.

By modeling and explaining skills such as cooperative learning, collaboration, and effective communication, both parents and teachers can help students develop the skill of teamwork in children. The following sections will explain ideas for both teachers and parents to help children learn this soft skill.

## HOW CAN EDUCATORS TEACH TEAMWORK TO CHILDREN?

Teamwork is a skill that is vital in the educational setting. Students are often called upon to create group projects, do experiments, and participate in activities such as peer editing and math workshops. Being able to work as a team in a learning environment is an important skill that all teachers should model and implement in their classroom.

Teaching and modeling the skill of teamwork is one that educators can implement from the first moment of class. Showing that the teacher values others and knows how to work appropriately with them is a skill that can be shown in all aspects of the school day. Modeling how one works with school colleagues, parents, students, and others is simple and easy to do. Being kind and respectful of others, promoting a positive learning environment, and displaying the characteristics of a *team player* can all go far in the classroom setting.

Creating a classroom that works as a team or community is another way to promote and teach the idea of teamwork in the classroom. Referring to the physical environment as "our classroom" and making the children feel welcome and valued allows a teacher to promote the soft skill of teamwork in a very valuable way. If students are included in activities such as creating rules, making decisions, and being responsible for the classroom, they will be more likely to feel like a part of the team environment.

Arranging cooperative learning groups in an intentional manner is also an effective way to teach teamwork in classrooms. Teachers who carefully and strategically select the placement of students in small groups will not only help children learn more effectively but should have improved classroom management as well. By separating certain students from each other and connecting others for collaboration, the teams will be more successful and the learning more focused.

Another idea for teaching teamwork in the classroom is to identify and teach social skills directly to the students. For example, when a teacher notices that there is conflict in groups or teams in the area of being kind and constructive when offering feedback, the teacher can complete a mini-lesson on how to communicate with others in the group, how to say comments in a kind way, and what to do if one disagrees with a group member. By teaching these skills and then watching for them in a group environment, students are more apt to learn the soft skill of teamwork in the classroom setting.

Group projects and team activities are often difficult because of the assessment involved. When teachers grade a project based solely on the product outcome, this can create havoc in the classroom when one student completes all of the work or when others are *slackers* (people who do little work and rely on others to do it). By grading both the final product and the cooperation involved, teachers will be able to assess both the project and the social aspect of getting along. This dual assessment can also provide feedback and opportunities for students to grow in the area of teamwork for future lessons.

Friendly competitions in the classroom are also a great way to teach teamwork. Often, teachers divide the students into "Table Teams" or "Work Groups" to enhance personal and group responsibility. Earning points for showing appropriate behavior, having a clean work area, and being ready to learn are excellent ways to involve students in an elementary setting. For older students, doing review activities, earning points for completing all components of an experiment, and teaching about the value of teamwork in class are all ways to motivate students to be better team players.

Reading novels and stories in which the characters have a problem that they must work together to solve is another way to teach teamwork in the classroom. Through this bibliotherapy approach, children can learn how teamwork is used by reading about it in the lives of others. Students of all ages are capable of empathizing with the characters in the book and identifying the teamwork skills used to resolve conflict or create a solution to a problem. A school or community librarian can assist teachers in finding developmentally appropriate books to reach this goal.

Discovering how others have worked together in the past is also a great way to teach about teamwork in the classroom. Historical figures such as explorers, civil rights leaders, and presidents have had to work together to promote a sense of community, solve problems, and make decisions that will impact others. Discussing the way that teamwork was used in such endeavors will share role models and exhibit the importance of teamwork in areas of history as well.

Having students interview adults in their lives about how they use teamwork in their jobs or other activities can explain why this is a vital soft skill for children to learn. By hearing from adults that this is a skill that is practiced in the workplace, faith-based groups, and community organizations, they will see that the teamwork activities taught in classrooms have a purpose for the creation of well-rounded, kind individuals who know how to work and care for others.

In conclusion, the skill of teamwork is one that children need to be successful in life. Whether they are working with a soccer team to score the next goal, a group of classmates to complete a school project, or an organization to complete a community service project, children need to learn how to work with others, collaborate for a common goal, and be successful in learning the skill of teamwork. Teamwork is a skill that will be needed in all areas of their future lives, both personal and professional. The following section will explain ways that parents can teach this skill as well.

## HOW CAN PARENTS TEACH TEAMWORK TO CHILDREN?

Parents can teach teamwork in a variety of ways, from encouraging children to participate in team activities to explaining the ways to work with others. Regardless of the path one chooses, teaching this skill is important for future success.

One of the first ways that children learn teamwork is through organized sports leagues. While these teams are an excellent way to encourage children to work together, they can also be challenging for students since they require effort, patience, and tact in children. Learning to wait for one's turn to participate, working together for a common goal, and relying on each other for *the good of the team* can teach children the skill of teamwork.

Sports teams can also model teamwork since children see parents and coaches working together. Parents who support the team and the coaches *without placing judgment and yelling at the coaches* can demonstrate that they support the teamwork that is being formed for the children. Sports leagues can also teach the important skills of being a humble winner and losing with grace and humility, characteristics that are often lacking in the real world.

Another way to encourage teamwork is through organizations such as scouting, school clubs, and faith-based activities. By working and learning together, children in such organizations can hone the skills of teamwork in activities, community service projects, and other ventures. Working with the same group each week enables children to gain the skills of negotiation, cooperation, and understanding. Not every child is the same, and learning to be patient with others and respect their differences in opinions is indeed a skill that all children need.

Teamwork in the family can also be taught by parents. Implementing the team model of parenting, with the idea that the parents are the coaches and the children are all part of the family team, is an innovative way to include children in the teamwork of family. Learning that everyone in the family must work together to respect others, do their share of the housework (including simple chores for young children), and make family-related decisions together can teach children how teamwork is valued—even at home.

While families today are very busy, taking the time to involve children in household decisions such as where to go on the next family vacation, how the family can work together to adopt a new pet, or ways that the family can support an ill relative will make children feel an important part of the family team. It will also help them realize the importance of working together, and such a skill is one that can be applied to more than just a sport or school activity.

A final way that families can teach teamwork is by sharing how this skill is used in the adult world. When parents have to work with an unkind coworker, deal with unruly neighbors, or cooperate with others in a group or organization, they can share the options they chose to use and show how teamwork and collaboration skills helped them to compromise and work together. Seeing that teamwork is a life skill that is used by adults on a daily basis will help children learn the importance and use of cooperation later in life.

In brief, learning the skill of teamwork and collaboration is one that can be started in a family setting, long before a child reaches school age. By working together in the home and participating in simple group activities such as sports teams and social groups, children will soon see that working together is an important life skill that they will need in future endeavors.

## KEY IDEAS

- Being able to work with others is an important soft skill for children to learn for future workplaces.
- Participating in team sports, group activities, and community service projects are all great ways for students to see and use teamwork in the real world.
- Creating a team environment where all classmates work together can help teachers educate students on the idea of teamwork.
- Carefully selecting groups for cooperative activities and teaching social skills are important ways to teach teamwork in the classroom setting.
- Considering how one teaches and assesses group projects is key to using this strategy in the classroom.
- Modeling teamwork in the family and home setting is a way for children to see how people work together.

# THREE

## Manners

- Why are manners important to teach to children?
- How can educators teach manners to children?
- How can parents teach manners to children?

### IMPORTANCE OF MANNERS

Manners are an important part of daily life. From being greeted in a warm way each morning, to saying "please" and "thank you" when receiving gifts, manners can make a child seem well-rounded and ready to meet the world. Manners are the way that one behaves around others. They include phrases such as "please," "thank you," and "excuse me," as well as actions such as respect and kindness.

Manners are not something that children are born with. They need to have the soft skill of manners taught and modeled for them by every adult in their lives. They also need to understand when *good* manners are used, as well as the impact of *bad* manners on others. Seeing how one uses manners on a daily basis is important for children beginning at a very early age.

From the time children learn to speak, they can be coached and expected to say, "please," "thank you," and "you're welcome" every time an item is given and received. By having these simple manners as an expectation in homes and classrooms, children will grow up with them as an automatic reaction and not something that is done just when company is present. Learning other phrases such as "excuse me" when walking in front of others or when one belches can be added when a child is ready.

Why are manners so important to children? It is because manners can exhibit a well-rounded, kind, and caring person. They show that the child acknowledges the feelings and needs of others and appreciates a helpful deed or kind action. Manners can exemplify a child who shows respect for rules and has learned the proper etiquette to survive in today's world. A child with good manners grows into an adult who is appreciated and respected in the workplace and other social settings.

Teaching children manners at an early age is a soft skill that is also a lifelong trait.

According to the website The Spruce.com (2019):

> Almost everyone understands that there's a reason for etiquette guide-lines and rules for good manners. After all, most parents start teaching polite words and phrases to their children early in life. They know that they're giving their children an advantage that will carry over into social, educational, and, eventually, professional situations.

By teaching children about manners at an early age, parents and educators are setting the stage for the requirements of being successful in the real world. Although some manners are outright and evident, others may be expected in social settings and in the workplace. By learning the soft skill of manners at an early age, children are apt to be more successful in their adult lives.

What is included in the skill of manners, and how can educators teach this in the classroom? The following will explain how to do this as well as some ways to model and teach this concept to children.

## HOW CAN EDUCATORS TEACH MANNERS TO CHILDREN?

In the classroom, manners are an important skill to teach and model. Teachers who expect manners and kindness for others in the classroom create classrooms that are kinder, safer, and have a sense of community. By beginning the school year with the expectation that the classroom is similar to a family and needs to be a place of kindness, support, and respect, the teacher can promote the idea of manners from day one.

A teacher is also important in the modeling and teaching of manners each day. Young children are very impressionable. If a student sees a teacher who is respectful and uses good manners, they are more likely to do so as well. At the same time, remembering that all students do not learn this skill at home is important too. Instead of becoming upset with a child who does not display good manners, taking the time to teach this skill and the importance of it is crucial in the development of such good manners.

Noticing and praising good manners and random acts of kindness in the classroom is another way for teachers to enhance the skill in their classrooms. When a child helps an injured child on the playground or assists a student who drops their tray in the cafeteria, noticing this kind behavior and saying, "Thank you for helping your friend. That was a very kind thing to do," can go a very long way. Children enjoy being praised and acknowledged when they exhibit kindness to others, and it is a great way to model the expectations in the classroom.

Acknowledging the work and service of others in the school building is also a way to teach manners in the classroom. A bus driver appreciation card, a thank you to the school secretary, or a nice note to the school custodian for cleaning the classroom every day are all ways to model manners and respect those who help the children on a daily basis. Students do not often see the work of the other people in a school setting, and learning to acknowledge them is a skill that children can take with them into the workplace as they obtain jobs and move to future careers.

Keeping the classroom neat and clean, taking care of school materials, and being respectful of people and their possessions are also important aspects of teaching manners. Because manners are not just words but actions, learning to respect the property of others and taking responsibility for the classroom are ways that all children can learn this skill in the classroom. Picking up toys at the end of recess for young children and cleaning the lab supplies after an experiment for older children are a few ways that a teacher can instruct students about manners through a sense of community in the classroom.

Overall, taking the time to teach and model manners can impact children throughout their entire lives. Many employers notice manners (or the lack of them) in job interviews. An applicant that greets an employer with a warm handshake, looks them in the eye, and uses good manners is one that will stand out in the mix of other interviewees. People who express kindness and use proper manners in an interview are likely to do the same in a work setting—and who would not like to have these people on their team?

## HOW CAN PARENTS TEACH MANNERS TO CHILDREN?

From the time children are able to speak, parents can begin modeling and teaching manners in the home. They can begin with "please," "thank you," and "you 're welcome" when someone gives a child a gift, when a server brings the food to the table at a restaurant, and when a friend pays them a compliment. Being aware of this basic step in manners is a great way to start, and it makes children seem kinder and more civil, simply with the use of a few basic words and phrases.

Teaching the first few phrases of manners can start by modeling with other family members. Parents who thank children for picking up toys, getting an item from the refrigerator, or showing kindness to others will raise children who do the same. Encouraging siblings and even visitors to the home to use these same manners can create an expectation that manners are used and expected in this child 's family and home.

Other manners, such as opening the door for an elderly person or a parent with a stroller or picking up an item dropped by someone at the library, can also be taught and modeled by parents. As children see kindness and behaviors toward others, they are likely to do the same actions when at a store or other public place.

Giving compliments to others is another great way to teach children manners. Learning to give genuine compliments when someone does a nice gesture, a kind deed, or even a mundane task can also model appropriate behaviors toward others. Thanking the mail carrier for delivering the mail, writing a note to the school bus driver at the end of the year, and noticing the services that people do for others is also a way to show appreciation and develop manners in children.

Thank you notes for birthday and holiday gifts are also a wonderful way to teach manners in children. Though this simple act is often forgotten in today 's world, it is a great skill for children to learn and one that is appreciated by gift givers and future employers. Having very young children draw a picture of the gift with an adult writing the dictated words of the child is an early way to develop this skill. As children get older, having an expectation that thank you notes are written is a way to teach the skill at home. In some homes, the children are not allowed to play with a new toy until a thank you is written—a great way to ensure that this is completed!

In today's world of technology, a text or video are also great ways to make sure that the giver is thanked without forcing children to write actual notes. A simple text to a grandparent for the birthday money and how it will be used is at least an effort to thank the parties involved. It may not be as formal as a written note, but it does teach the skill and expectation of acknowledging a gift and the gift giver. It also lets long-distance givers know that the gift was received and appreciated.

Another way to thank a gift giver is a quick video of the child opening the gift or playing with the new item. "Thanks for the new book, Aunt Sue" accompanied by the child reading a few pages is a welcome element for a gift giver and allows the person to see the joy in the child using the gift they sent. In other words, it is not the actual *note* that makes the difference here. It is acknowledging the gift was received and that the child appreciates the gift and thoughtfulness involved by the sender.

Aside from the basic ideas of please and thank you, manners can be taught in other ways as well. Picking up one's toys after a play date, helping with dishes after meals, and refraining from texting at the dinner table are also important for teaching good manners. Looking a person in the eye while speaking and offering a handshake when meeting new people also matter.

In general, simply modeling and teaching the ideas of kindness and respect to others, being responsible for picking up clothes and other possessions, and noticing when someone else shows kindness to others can go a long way in teaching manners to children. While this skill alone could take chapters to write, the important idea here is that manners are embedded in the daily lives of children and are expected in the home and public places.

As Pam Myers, author of *The Importance of Teaching Manners to Kids* (2019), states:

> You do your children such a big favor when you teach them good manners. From bosses to girlfriends, good manners can make or break an opportunity. For instance, if your child is up for his first job and his credentials match another candidate's, the more polite and mannerly candidate may end up with the job.

Teaching manners to children at an early age will help them be respectful, kind, and noticed. People notice children who act appropriately, use kind manners, and exhibit this skill to others. By working on manners both at school and at home, teachers and parents can help raise a generation of children who are polite and kind.

## KEY POINTS

- Manners begin with simple words and phrases such as "please," "thank you," and "you're welcome."
- Not all children learn manners at home. Being able to teach them in school is important for teachers to do.
- Manners also include actions such as opening doors for others, cleaning up the toys after a play date, and helping others in need.
- Parents and teachers can both teach manners to children by modeling and expecting them on a daily basis.
- Manners also include items such as sending thank you notes, avoiding texting at the dinner table, and acknowledging the help and assistance of others.
- Manners are a soft skill that is noticed by others and can help with social skills, educational endeavors, and even future job settings.

# FOUR

## Respect

- Why is respect an important skill to teach children?
- How can educators teach the skill of respect to children?
- How can parents teach the skill of respect to children?

IMPORTANCE OF RESPECT

Respect can be a difficult concept to explain to children. It is a term that adults frequently use but often do not take the time to define in words that children can identify with. However, defining this term in simple, child-friendly terms is an important start to teaching this soft skill to children. According to Talking Tree Books (2019): "Respect is a big concept to grasp. Try this definition of respect for kids, written in terms children can understand, and with examples of what is respect for others and what is respect for self. A definition of respect includes 1) how you feel about someone, and 2) how you treat him/her."

Learning to respect oneself and others is a characteristic that is often defined by actions rather than words. Children learn the soft skill of respect by watching adults in their everyday interactions and how they treat others. Respect is showing kindness to others when helping an older person or treating someone in a thoughtful way when there is conflict. Children learn respect when they see how their parents handle stressful situations or show compassion to someone that they encounter.

Respect is a way of life in many households and classrooms when children treat each other with care and concern. They show empathy when they see others with problems or concerns and are caring, kind, and helpful. It is also seen when children do compassionate deeds and show actions that are thoughtful of others. Respect is also apparent through the use of good manners and proper actions.

Respect is also seen in children who practice the skill of self-respect. Self-respect, according to Cambridge Dictionary.com (2019) is "1) a feeling of respect for yourself that shows that you value yourself, and 2) positive thoughts and feelings about yourself; self-esteem." Children who have respect for themselves and think positively about themselves are apt to show more respect to others.

The famous saying by author Leo Buscaglia (2019)—"To love others you must first love yourself"—is very true in teaching the concept of respect to children. If children are not taught the idea of self-respect and valuing self, it will be very difficult to practice the skill of respect with others. One must start with pride and satisfaction with one's self to show the skill of love and caring for others. Working on self-esteem and self-care are both great ways that adults can begin teaching this skill to children.

Teaching self-respect involves teaching children to have pride in their work, taking care of their possessions, and having an attitude of caring and concern about their overall well-being. Teaching children to be humble, gracious, and genuine when they do well are also included in this skill. Being able to be both a winner and a loser without bragging, boasting, and saying hurtful things shows not only self-respect but also respect to others.

Taking care of one's health, cleanliness, and hygiene are also important keys to self-respect. Taking care of one's possessions, being clean and healthy, and promoting a lifestyle of healthy habits are all important skills in learning to value self in children. Avoiding negative people and unhealthy habits, taking care of one's property, and practicing self-respect on a daily basis are the keys to learning to respect others.

By first learning the skill of self-respect, children will be ready to respect others. Respecting others is a skill that both teachers and parents can teach to children in their care. By showing concern and caring for the well-being of children, allowing them to have ownership and decision-making opportunities, and modeling respect for others, teachers and parents can show children that the skill of respect is an important one. The next section will explain ways that teachers can enhance this skill in the classroom.

## HOW CAN EDUCATORS TEACH RESPECT TO CHILDREN?

Teachers help children learn the soft skill of respect in schools and classrooms. Many teachers begin the school year with teaching students about rules and procedures, several of which may involve the idea of respect in some way. Modeling skills such as taking turns and sharing toys shows even the youngest children how to implement this skill in the classroom.

Beginning the school year with activities that promote both self-esteem and respect to others are ways that teachers can promote this skill in the classroom. Teaching children to take care of themselves and their property are important items to consider when working with a new class of students. Talking about what it means to have self-respect and show kindness to others in the form of good deeds, a caring environment, and a considerate classroom are all strategies that are easy to teach and helpful to all.

Having class mottos and expectations of treating others with respect or *respecting self, people, and property* are all simple ways that teachers can explain and teach this disposition in the school setting. Creating a sense of community in the classroom and teaching children the importance of caring will help develop a kind and compassionate classroom of students.

Reading books about characters who are kind, respectful, and make good decisions is another way that teachers can promote respect in the classroom. Discussing the actions of the characters and how their actions impacted others will model the idea of respect through reading and apply this skill to real-life situations. Students who are surrounded by good role models—both real and fictional—will learn about appropriate behaviors and the importance of treating others with kindness and respect.

Taking care of issues such as teasing and bullying in a swift manner is also a way that teachers can instill respect in their students. Instead of ignoring problems such as arguments between children, unkind words, or other unpleasant situations, teachers who turn these events into teachable moments will be able to explain, model, and instruct students about how to better handle such situations in the future. Asking children how they would feel if the tables were turned can help them empathize with other students and learn to think about their actions before doing them.

Class meetings that deal with disrespectful situations or altercations in the classroom is a way for teachers to deal with problems that can occur. Having a class meeting in which the children are allowed to voice opinions, listen to others, and brainstorm possible solutions helps model a respectful classroom where others are valued and respected. By allowing students ownership and rights in the classroom, a teacher models the respect they have for the students and develops a sense of family and community among the children.

Older students can be shown respect in the classroom as they earn more rights and privileges when they show maturity and responsibility. By noticing the proper behaviors and actions of students, a teacher can reward such behavior by allowing the students a bit more freedom and autonomy than they once had. Older students appreciate and acknowledge when teachers are respectful of them and will return this respect in kind.

Supporting the strengths and talents of individual students will also help teachers enhance the skill of self-respect in the classroom. Teachers who concentrate on the talents of children and assist them in strengthening the skills they are lacking will help the students to see that they are important and valuable to others. By developing the skill of self-respect, teachers can help the students learn to respect others.

Activities that promote the abilities and talents of children and are differentiated to meet their needs are strategies that teachers can use to promote both self-respect and respect for others in the classroom. Learning that all children are different and allowing students to explore interest areas, hobbies, and areas of strength are all ways that teachers can enhance the self-esteem in children while also promoting the respect of different abilities, values, and cultures.

By allowing children to concentrate on their strengths, collaborate with others, and truly learn to value the abilities and differences of others, teachers can help both individual students and the classroom as a whole. Learning to respect classmates and working together on both areas of strength and deficits can promote an admirable learning environment where children learn to love themselves and appreciate others with whom they learn.

Allowing children to interact with children who have disabilities and creating an atmosphere of acceptance is another key to learning respect in the classroom. With the creation of inclusionary classrooms, students are more apt to accept and learn about the needs of others and learn to respect them—both in and out of school. Working with children in a classroom setting means that teachers can set the tone for a loving, caring environment of learning in which *all* children are accepted and taught in respectful ways.

In brief, educators play an important role in the development of respect in children. Teachers who are respectful of children, model and teach kindness, and encourage their students to show compassion and empathy will create classrooms that are community-oriented and places where children can grow. Educators who teach the skill of self-respect will mold children into adults who are well-balanced and accepting of others. By working together with parents, teachers can accommodate children, model appropriate behaviors, and develop a skill that will last a lifetime.

## HOW CAN PARENTS TEACH RESPECT TO CHILDREN?

Parents can begin teaching the soft skill of respect to children by first modeling this skill in the home. Parents who are kind and loving to each other and the other members of a family are the first way that children see this behavior modeled for them. Showing caring behaviors and expecting this from all members of the household is a great beginning. Even though parents and siblings might disagree with each other, they can still be taught to demonstrate the characteristics of respect. Families argue, disagree, and even fight on occasion; however, learning how to handle these disagreements in a respectful manner is key to the development of this skill for children.

Modeling and teaching kindness and respect to others is also a way that parents can teach this skill to children. Demonstrating kindness and manners to others through actions such as opening doors, saying "excuse me," and extending a hand to those in need are all simple but valuable ways to do this.

Helping a stranger who drops their groceries in a store, assisting a neighbor with raking the leaves, or taking dinner to an ill friend are all respectful actions and can teach about caring and concern for others.

Treating others (even strangers) with respect shows children that exhibiting kindness and caring are skills that take very little effort but can make others feel loved and appreciated. Also, helping others often makes us have a positive feeling—simply because seeing another person smile and be thankful for our help just makes us feel good.

Respect can also be taught by parents when their children see them in stressful situations. How a parent handles themselves in situations such as a traffic jam, with a disrespectful person at the grocery store, or an unruly neighbor are all ways that children can witness the skill of respect in the family. When parents react with anger or with inappropriate words and actions, children will see this and often mimic the same actions in later situations. However, if parents can model such circumstances with grace and dignity, children can learn that respect can help de-escalate situations as well.

We all make mistakes. Even the server who brings the wrong food, the person who doesn't use a turn signal while driving, and the clerk who rings up the wrong item are all worthy of forgiveness. Modeling kindness and respect are ways that children watch parents display this behavior. Instead of cussing and swearing or being unkind and threatening, parents can kindly ask for a new item, explain a problem in a calm way, and in turn model respect—even in stressful situations.

Parents can also model and teach respect by displaying this skill to others. Many years ago, children were taught to respect elders and to respect authority figures. However, this is not always modeled in today's homes. Teaching children to respect their teachers, coaches, and authority figures such as police officers is an important part of teaching respect to others. Even when parents disagree with these people, it is key to take care of problems or concerns in a respectful and kind manner. Children are watching how parents handle certain issues and not putting children in the middle of such actions is important for parents to remember.

Remembering that respect is *earned* and not an automatic action is the vital component of this skill. Parents who model kindness and compassion to others will raise children who use respect in their homes and in other venues. At the same time, parents who model unkind words and actions will raise children who use these actions as well.

Finally, promoting the skill of self-respect is important in the home. Parents need to teach children to have positive thoughts and to love and accept themselves as they are. Having realistic expectations, teaching children to be humble, and helping children to have a balance between bragging and being proud are all components of this skill. All children have bad days, bring home a poor test grade, or go through phases where they don't love their appearance, but teaching children to appreciate who they are and accept those bad days in life will help teach about self-respect.

Children also have great days when they bring home a good report card, hit a home run, or perform a dance in the school musical. Praising children and showing pride in them are ways that parents can help with self-esteem, but allowing children to brag or boast too much can hinder the development of self-respect in children. Teaching an appropriate level of self-respect that is positive without being unkind is a way that parents can help with this skill. Since self-respect is the basis for learning to respect others, learning this skill at an early age is vital to the development of children.

Overall, the skill of respect is one that is first modeled and taught in the home. Having families that exhibit respect in the household by helping others, being positive, and showing empathy will produce children who are kind to others, including classmates and future co-workers. Being respectful is a characteristic that is noticed by teachers, employers, and others. When one is treated with respect and kindness, it is remembered by all.

### KEY IDEAS

- Respect is the way that one thinks about others and how one treats them.
- Teachers can model the skill of respect to children by showing compassion and kindness as well as how they treat others in stressful situations.
- Respect is earned. The more one respects others, the more one is respected.
- Teaching self-respect is also an important skill for children to learn.
- Parents can also teach and model respect at home by showing kindness and caring to others.
- Both groups—parents and teachers—can help children learn respect. This is a skill that is noticed and appreciated by others in school and in future job settings.

# FIVE

## Empathy

- Why is empathy an important skill for children?
- How can educators teach the skill of empathy to children?
- How can parents teach the skill of empathy to children?

### IMPORTANCE OF EMPATHY

Empathy is an important soft skill for children to learn, both at home and at school. Learning to emulate how others think and how one's feelings impact their decisions can help children develop this soft skill in their formative years. According to Lawrence Kutner, author of *How Children Develop Empathy* (2018):

> To empathize with someone is to understand what he is feeling or, more properly, to understand what you would feel like if you were in his situation. It is an extension of self-concept, but it is far more complex. It requires an awareness that others think of themselves in ways that are both similar to and different from the way you do, and that they also have emotions they associate with those thoughts and images.

Empathy in children can be a tricky skill to teach. It is not something one learns in a parenting class or a college course. It is a spur-of-the-moment skill that children cultivate over time as they witness the emotions of others and try to imagine how they are feeling at that moment. Empathy is a developmental skill that takes time and maturity to learn. A kindergarten student will not have the same depth of empathy as a high school senior.

Children learn empathy when problems occur, a friend gets hurt, or a happy event takes place. They learn to put themselves into the situation to try to see how the other person feels and why their reactions match those feelings. They also learn empathy when others are kind and caring. When a friend helps after a fall on the playground or a classmate offers a listening ear in a high school class, students learn that empathy is a skill that will make them better people.

Media and social media are also ways that model compassion, or even poor decisions, made by people in the news. Children see both caring acts and unkind deeds happen in the wake of media outlets. They often question why bad things happen to good people and want to know why individuals make the decisions that they do. However, instead of dismissing an awkward question at the dinner table or during a classroom meeting, adults can take these opportunities to teach the skill of empathy and help children learn how people feel in these situations.

Empathy is also an important life skill that can take one far in a future career. People who are well-rounded in the area of empathy work well with others, both in school and in the workforce. Knowing how others feel and putting one's self in their place will enable people to be more kind and caring as life happens around them. Teaching this soft skill to kids will help them learn as children and will enable them to be well-rounded adults in the future. The following section will explain how teachers can help teach this skill in their classrooms.

## HOW CAN EDUCATORS TEACH EMPATHY TO CHILDREN?

Teachers play an important role in developing empathy in children. They are in classrooms on a daily basis and can teach and explain situations in which empathy matters. How a teacher reacts to a child who is ill, whose feelings are hurt, or who is dealing with a difficult home life can impact how students in the classroom react to these events. Children know when someone in the classroom is struggling. Watching the teacher handle these situations can model the soft skill of empathy.

Using the phrase "How would you feel if that happened to you"? is also a beneficial skill to use in the classroom. Children often make spontaneous decisions without thinking about how something will impact others. Simply reversing the roles and asking about the feelings and actions of others can be a great way to teach this skill to children.

Every day in classrooms across the world, teachers encounter situations in which children get hurt, make poor choices, and see unkind deeds. It is not because children are innately *bad*; it is simply because they do not know how to handle such situations in an adult way. Taking the time to explain how one's actions impact others and how one would feel in the same situation is a great way for teachers to develop empathy in their classrooms.

Asking about the feelings of others is also a skill that can be used in the content one is teaching. When reading about a character who is treated unkindly, asking how the children would feel in the same situation is a skillful way to teach empathy in the content that is already required.

Using this same approach with people in history who were treated unfairly is also a tool for teaching empathy. Many people in the history of the world were not treated with kind words or had bad things happen to them. Allowing students to focus on the reactions of others and how they were treated can introduce empathy with real characters and actions.

Completing service opportunities such as volunteering or collecting items for others is another great way to teach empathy in the classroom. Volunteering to help with younger children at the school or collecting items for a local food pantry can enable students to learn the needs of others and create compassionate people as a result. By putting others first and considering their feelings, students will see that even children can make a difference.

Learning about community needs, advocating for the environment, and helping with social justice causes can help children learn empathy in the classroom as well. Discussing how throwing trash on the ground or adding pollution to the water is bad helps children learn how their poor choices impact those around them and allows them to advocate for a good cause, which can lead to children empathizing with others. As long as a teacher has administrative permission for any controversial ideas, this will also help children perfect the soft skill of empathy.

In all, empathy is an important soft skill for children of all ages. By learning empathy, they will be able to put themselves in another person's place, explain how others may feel in similar situations, and hopefully learn to be caring and compassionate as a result. Children learn empathy through the relationships they have with others, and parents and educators play a major role in this learning.

Children who learn empathy at an early age are apt to be more kind and caring with others in their schools and social activities. However, one of the most important keys to this soft skill is that teaching empathy to students will allow them to carry this behavior into the adult world of college, careers, and civic engagement. Empathetic children become caring co-workers and kind employees when they reach adulthood, and that will make the world a better place!

## HOW CAN PARENTS TEACH EMPATHY TO CHILDREN?

Empathy is not a skill that children are born with. They learn it through watching others, being in certain situations, and seeing how people handle real-life situations. As Lawrence Kutner, author of *How Children Develop Empathy*, put it:

> Unlike intelligence and physical attractiveness, which depend largely on genetics, empathy is a skill that children learn. Its value is multifold. Children who are empathic tend to do better in school, in social situations, and in their adult careers. Children and teenagers who have the greatest amount of skill at empathy are viewed as leaders by their peers. The best teachers of that skill are the children's parents.

Empathy is often learned by watching one's parents handle difficult situations and how they deal with the feelings of others. It is a soft skill that children develop over time, and families are probably one of the most influential aspects of how this skill is learned. Children watch their parents and model their empathy after them. Teaching this skill to one's children can happen in many ways.

First, empathy is developed when one witnesses acts of caring and compassion. Watching a parent help a friend in need, having an adult who does caring deeds, and talking with them about why they made the choices they did can enable a child to become more empathetic. When a friend is ill and a parent makes dinner or runs errands to help, they are modeling empathy and compassion to their children. When a co-worker gets behind on a project and a parent offers to help so that she can attend her child's ball game, children see empathy happening before them.

By modeling and encouraging compassionate acts, children can see how kindness can help others. When a friend loses a grandparent, a child can make a card and learn that the words "I'm sorry" can go a very long way. Teaching children that empathy can be shown through one's words and actions is a key skill for children to learn for the future.

Working with people who have disabilities, volunteering to help collect items for hurricane victims, and helping an elderly neighbor with her gardening are also ways that parents can teach and encourage empathy. Even young children can help with these efforts, alongside their parents and siblings. By doing so, little ones can learn the importance of empathy and compassion with people who are in need.

Various media are also prevalent in today's homes. Watching the television in the evening with the family, a child can learn empathy by discussing how a character must have felt in a movie or television program. Also, monitoring social media and being aware of situations where cyberbullying has taken place are opportunities for teenagers to discuss these problems with their parents. Allowing teenagers to voice their opinions and come up with better solutions will enable them to practice the skill of empathy through teachable moments in the household.

Reading books to children at bedtime is an event that happens in many households. It is calming and allows a parent to build relationships with their children while doing so. However, it can also be used as an opportunity to develop empathy as well. Stopping during the story to ask how the character feels and what the child would do in such a situation can build empathy with very little effort. It simply takes a few minutes of time and some careful thought to ask the questions that will help guide children in this area.

By modeling and teaching empathy to children, parents can create children who are understanding, compassionate, and caring. Kids look up to the adults in their lives, and parents are the first people to show them how empathy works. They model how to help other people in difficult situations and answer questions about challenging topics. This skill, in turn, will be beneficial as these children enter the real world of work and society. A kind and empathetic co-worker is something every future employee would like to see in the workplace.

## KEY IDEAS

- Empathy is a skill that children are not born with. It is a skill that they learn and develop over time.

- Children learn empathy through watching others. They watch the parents and teachers in their lives and model their behaviors on them.
- Difficult situations are oftentimes where students learn the most empathy. Taking the time to discuss these with children is important.
- Volunteering, helping others in times of need, and doing kind deeds can help even young children learn the skill of empathy.
- Children develop empathy in all settings, including classrooms and homes. Realizing that empathy can be taught in any situation is key.
- By teaching and modeling empathy in children, parents and teachers create adults who will go far in their future careers.

# SIX

## Composure

- Why is composure important to children?
- How can educators teach the skill of composure to children?
- How can parents teach the skill of composure to children?

### IMPORTANCE OF COMPOSURE

Composure, according to a recent edition of *Psychology Today*, is "the ability to remain calm yet focused under pressure" (Nemko, 2018). When someone gets upset by the actions of others, a problem at home, or a situation at school, they are apt to become angry; it is human nature. However, it is how one handles that anger that is important. Becoming angry but being able to remain calm and focused is the key to composure.

We see composure around us every day. The gymnast who takes the floor in the Olympics and never looks nervous is showing composure. A father in the grocery store who has three screaming children yet remains calm, cool, and collected is modeling composure. The teacher who sees a child injured on the playground yet calmly handles the situation shows composure as well.

Getting angry is a part of growing up. Kids see or hear things that make them upset. They get into arguments with siblings and have disagreements on the playground. However, being able to handle this anger in an appropriate way is the key to learning composure. A composed child works out problems rather than holds grudges. A composed child uses problem-solving instead of yelling unkind words, and a composed child learns a sense of compassion and kindness in dealing with problem situations.

Composure is also learning to deal with emotions and outbursts in an appropriate way. Rather than throwing a fit or tantrum when another child will not share her toys, a composed child will ask kindly and learn to take turns. A child who exhibits composure will also be able to use self-soothing techniques that will be able to de-escalate the anger to a minimal level. Being able to count to ten, for example, can teach a child to step back, examine the problem, and not act hastily.

Composure is a soft skill that is needed both at home and school. At home, children must interact with others in the family, including parents, siblings, and even pets. When a child interacts with others on a daily basis, tension is bound to happen. Simply living in the same environment, day in and day out, with the same people, makes that friction occur. However, learning how to deal with this tension can help children learn composure at home.

Conflict also occurs at school, whether that conflict occurs with others or internally. Children may have disagreements, arguments, and conflict with peers over projects, group structures, and viewpoints. They may also have internal conflict when they struggle with the course material, forget to complete homework, or are just having a bad day. Learning ways to remain calm, focused, and relaxed in the midst of such conflict is the key to composure.

The following sections will explain ways that teachers and parents can model the soft skill of composure. Learning this skill will help in all areas of life, whether it is during a sporting event, a speech one must make for school, or in the work setting when presenting a proposal to one's boss. Composure is a tool that is needed in life and a skill that will be needed in childhood and beyond.

## HOW CAN EDUCATORS TEACH COMPOSURE TO CHILDREN?

Educators can begin by modeling the skill of composure to children outside the home. When a schedule changes, a child misbehaves, or a computer stops working, teachers need to model a calm and collected attitude with the children. According to author and educator Annette Breaux, "It's not our feelings that determine who we are to others, but rather our actions. And one of the most difficult tasks to accomplish as a teacher is the ability to control your actions and maintain your composure at all costs" (Breaux, 2013).

A teacher who remains calm in the middle of a confrontation, speaks kindly to an upset parent, and deals with problems appropriately is one that models composure to children in their classroom. A teacher who can take a school situation such as a weather delay or school intruder drill and remain calm and composed will model both a calm and safe environment for children. Focusing on remaining calm models for students that they are safe and that the adults are in control of such situations. The ability to do this is an asset to both a school and the students.

Talking about people who have faced problems or adversity, both in history and the present, can help students understand the skill of composure as well. A historical figure who had to make difficult decisions, rely on others, and use decision-making skills can be shared as an example of a person who showed composure even under fire. A character in a book can also become the focus of a group discussion when she faces bullying or another stressful situation. Equipping students with the knowledge of how others overcame problems or handled stressful situations are excellent ways for making this skill more realistic to children.

Working with the school counselor, school nurse, parents, and others is also beneficial in helping children learn composure. A school counselor can help children who are overly sensitive or worry about problems more than they should. A school nurse can teach about the physical effects of stress on the body, and parents can help work alongside teachers if a child has extreme issues such as panic attacks or tantrums. Working together with all parties involved in a child's life represents a community of people who want to help children remain safe and learn to be less stressed and focused.

Teaching self-soothing skills with early learners and stress management techniques with older students is another way that teachers can successfully teach composure in the classroom. Taking a brain break when the classroom instruction gets overwhelming, teaching children to take deep breaths and focus on their learning, and teaching problem-solving skills to students are also valuable. If a child can learn to take care of himself and manage stress, he will be more likely to handle high-pressure situations, and he will be more ready for the real-life stressors he may encounter further down the road.

Composure is a skill that is needed by both children and adults. It is about how one handles the stressors in life that can make a difference in how one handles problems and adversity in the future. By learning to be composed as children, students will learn to use this skill in their college studies and future careers as well. The next section will explain how parents can teach this skill at home.

## HOW CAN PARENTS TEACH COMPOSURE TO CHILDREN?

The first way that parents can teach composure in the home is by modeling it. Accidents happen, stressful things take place, and everyday problems ensue. Milk gets spilled, traffic gets backed up, and things get broken. However, it is how parents handle problems such as the spilled drink, the traffic jam, or the broken item that is important to the children who are watching.

A parent who takes control of the situation by cleaning up the spill or broken glass swiftly but without losing her cool is the parent that is modeling composure for her children. The father who takes the traffic jam or broken lawnmower in stride is also modeling composure. However, a parent who yells, swears, and loses control not only does actions without thinking but also models these actions to children.

According to Pam Nicholson, author of *Staying Calm During the Storm* (2019):

> When parents model assertiveness and calmness, children can learn how to manage their own angry feelings in a constructive and effective way. With an attitude of acceptance toward the inevitability of anger, with some techniques in mind, and with conscious effort on your part to stay cool, you can help your children learn to manage, in a healthy way, the anger that is an expected and normal part of the human experience.

Anger is a common human emotion. Everyone has events or problems that make them angry. However, by learning the skill of composure, children will learn how to deal with this appropriately to remain calm and focused.

Stress and anxiety are also areas where composure is needed to be successful. Dancing in a recital, participating in a competition, or playing in a sporting event are fun but often nerve-wracking events. It is great to be the lead dancer in the school performance, but it is also a stressful situation. Competing in a school debate is interesting but can also cause anxiety. Throwing the game-winning free throw is exciting but is also a daunting task. Teaching children how to practice calmness and stay focused can help them be successful without falling prey to nerves.

Practicing both the skills involved, such as the dance moves needed and free throws in the backyard, can certainly help a child be prepared for competitive situations, but it also teaches the skills of being a humble winner and graceful loser, which are also important components in teaching composure to children. When children win a game or competition, for example, remembering to not become boastful and condescending to others is important. At the same time, learning to be a graceful loser is important as well. We can't win every game. However, by learning these skills, we will learn the appropriate ways to both win and lose in the future.

Teaching children relaxation techniques such as deep breathing, counting to ten, and focusing on the task at hand can also help children learn the skill of composure. Reminding children to schedule time for fun and relaxation is also helpful. While dance and debate may be great skills to learn, children also need to be encouraged to relax and put their feet up.

Hearing an adult's examples of a past problem that was difficult to manage can also help children learn about composure. Learning about the ways an adult handled such issues can help children form their own coping strategies. By helping them understand that everyone has problems and stressful situations in their lives, children can see that composure is a soft skill that is needed and used in their everyday lives.

Responding to children's temper tantrums and anger in an appropriate way is another way to help teach and model composure in the home and in public. If a child throws a fit in a public place, either ignoring the behavior or talking in a calm, quiet manner can help the situation. Parents who scream and lose control of their own emotions will model this behavior to their children and will likely raise ones who mimic the same behaviors in the future.

Using the term *composure* and pointing out examples of it are also great ways to teach this skill in the home. When the athlete on television is about to take the game-winning putt, pointing this out to children and talking about ways that the person uses composure to breathe, concentrate, and focus is a useful life skill. Seeing a character in a movie that is under pressure can create a productive conversation about how they remained calm even in the midst of adversity.

All of these skills can help a child not only see the importance of composure in life but also how to attain this skill as well. By working together, teachers and parents can help children learn how to handle emotions and how to develop the skill of composure. Teaching children that it is acceptable to get angry is fine. However, teaching them how to deal with this and remain calm is even better!

## KEY IDEAS

- Composure is the ability to stay calm and focused under pressure.
- All people have problems, experience stress, and have accidents. It's how one handles these situations that is important.
- Parents and teachers model composure when bad things occur, and they handle them with calmness and humility.
- Looking at characters and real people who are under pressure and discussing how they handle such situations can also teach the skill of composure.
- Learning stress relief techniques and ways to decrease anxiety are excellent strategies to help children learn composure.
- All adults in a child's life can help teach the skill of composure.

# SEVEN

# Responsibility

- Why is responsibility important to children?
- How can educators teach the skill of responsibility?
- How can parents teach the skill of responsibility?

## IMPORTANCE OF RESPONSIBILITY

Responsibility is a soft skill that helps children learn to be accountable, dependable, and conscientious. Responsibility helps children see that their actions and deeds impact others and helps them realize that doing their share of the work makes them accountable to others. Responsibility begins at an early age and can allow children to develop a skill that they will use for the rest of their lives.

Being responsible implies that a student does what they are told, follows through with commitments, and does their part to contribute to an assignment or project. Teaching kids responsibility means that there are rewards and consequences for getting things done and that someone will be checking on the progress and completion of certain tasks. Having a parent or teacher check on the progress of chores, assignments, and other commitments mean that a child will be held accountable for his or her actions and workload.

Children who learn responsibility at home will be more likely to continue this skill at school and in their future workplace. By learning the skill of follow-through and accountability, students will discover that their work is important and that other people rely on them to complete tasks that are assigned to them. As former advice columnist Abigail Van Buren (of Dear Abby fame) put it, "If you want children to keep their feet on the ground, put some responsibility on their shoulders" (Van Buren, no date).

By learning to shoulder some responsibility from a young age, children will see the importance of doing their part, learn that they are part of a larger community, and find that following through with chores and assignments is an expectation to be successful in the world. Both teachers and parents can help children learn responsibility, and this soft skill should be a part of every classroom and home.

Teachers who encourage the soft skill of responsibility are those who assign tasks, expect actions, and hold children accountable for their accomplishments. The following section will examine how teachers can help children learn this skill in the classroom.

## HOW CAN EDUCATORS TEACH RESPONSIBILITY TO CHILDREN?

Teachers are an important factor in teaching responsibility to children. They can show children the importance of this skill, model it in the classroom setting, and hold children accountable for their actions. Teaching about the importance of homework, doing one's part on class projects, and making students responsible for their own actions is a vital skill that all children need to learn.

Educators can teach the skill of responsibility by having class chores such as paper passer, line leader, and class pet feeder. By having roles and responsibilities for the children, teachers can build trust in students, explain the importance of follow-through, and teach students about a sense of community in the classroom. If all students have a job and must do their part, they will learn the meaning of working together and the importance of relying on each other to meet goals and expectations.

Teaching students about the skill of responsibility will allow them to see the importance of this trait in the real world and will prepare them for future jobs and obligations. All people in a society have roles they must do, responsibilities that they must undertake, and tasks that are needed to survive. By teaching children responsibility in the classroom, teachers are preparing their students to be successful in life. According to the website Proud to be Primary (2019): "Teaching responsibility in the classroom is important. By teaching your students to be responsible in the classroom, you're also teaching them to be responsible at home and in their communities. This is a life skill that they will need to practice throughout their lives."

Another way that educators can teach responsibility is simply creating an atmosphere of family and community in the classroom. By creating this type of environment, teachers model that the classroom is everyone's responsibility. Therefore, at the end of the day, *all* students should clean up the classroom, picking up trash on the floor—even if it does not belong to them. Having a community environment also teaches students that they need to work together, help each other, and be accountable for doing one's best, all with the idea that the classroom must work together to succeed.

Emphasizing responsibility in group projects, class commitments, and other undertakings is also a way that teachers can teach this soft skill in the classroom. By doing mini-lessons about responsibility, having discussions about what happens when one does not pull their weight, and talking about how others feel when a student is irresponsible, students can learn firsthand how responsibility impacts both themselves and others.

Dividing the workload accordingly, creating schedules and check-ins, and monitoring the progress of small groups all allow the teacher to check on the responsibility of projects and other class endeavors. From kindergarten to high school, children need to see that being a responsible group member is an important skill to have, and those who develop this skill in the early years will become co-workers who follow through with their responsibilities later in life.

A final way that educators can teach responsibility is by expecting that children complete homework, are on time for assignments, and have due dates and expectations for them in the classroom. By establishing such procedures in the classroom, students will know exactly when items are due, will have clear expectations for assignments, and will understand the consequences of being late.

By deducting a few points for late or unfinished assignments, educators are teaching about the importance of responsibility and follow through in the classroom. Starting in upper elementary grades, through high school, students need to learn that being on time is included in the responsibility of homework assignments. Losing a few points for a late penalty teaches children that timeliness is a part of this responsibility as well.

Having policies for turning in late work is an important procedure for the teacher to provide. For example, if a child is ill (or has an excused absence), giving them the number of days absent to complete assignments is a policy that many teachers use. Therefore, if a child is ill for three days, he has three extra days to complete the make-up work without a late penalty. By having procedures in place, teachers have a plan and can communicate these expectations to parents as well.

In the real world, employees are expected to complete jobs and assignments on time. If not, a penalty may be applied, or a person could even lose her job. Adults are expected to pay their bills on time as well. If they don't, a late fee is typically added to the original bill. By modeling this real-life responsibility of a penalty for being late in the classroom, teachers will be doing their part to prepare students for this soft skill in the future.

For children who are habitually late with assignments, teachers and parents may need to correspond with an extra layer of communication. A parent-teacher conference with the child in attendance might be needed to help explain responsibility and create a plan of action. An extra note or assignment notebook may be needed that a teacher signs each afternoon and that a parent reads each evening. For older students, an electronic format such as a gradebook or planner that parents can assess may help a young adult to work on due dates and expectations.

By working together, educators and parents can teach the skill of responsibility to children. Creating both home and school environments where everyone has a role and is accountable is a great way to start. Teaching children about responsibility and helping them learn about commitments to teams, classmates, and others is an important part of this skill. However, teaching this skill at home is just as important. The next section will explain how parents can teach this skill as well.

HOW CAN PARENTS TEACH RESPONSIBILITY TO CHILDREN?

Parents can begin teaching responsibility to children at a very young age. From the time children are walking and playing, they can be taught to pick up toys and put them back where they belong. Simple skills such as putting things back in their place can be taught as family expectations.

Contributing to the family and having family expectations and chores is also a way for children to learn responsibility in the home. Even the youngest of children can have family chores and show their responsibility and accountability in the household. Young children can set the table, put things away, and help with grocery lists. They can help with the family pets, sweep the sidewalks, and put their clothes away.

Expecting children to help without expecting perfection is the key to teaching young children responsibility. Remembering that they can help with chores and everyday jobs is great. However, remembering that their work may not be perfect is a major key for teaching responsibility at a young age. If a child is supposed to set the table, for example, they may not have the forks in the exact location and the napkins in the correct place concerning etiquette, but the simple fact that the forks and napkins arrived at the table is the point.

Sometimes adults set the bar a little too high for children. However, noting that we all started somewhere is an important point to remember. If children make an effort, try to do their best, and follow through with what they are told, it is a great start in teaching responsibility. As they continue to do the skill and gain some maturity, they will get better at the chores assigned to them and will gain self-confidence as a contributing member of the family.

Teaching children about other obligations such as homework and team or club commitments is another part of gaining responsibility. Instructing students about the importance of homework and teaching them a simple routine in the evening will help them learn this skill as a family. Also, learning that being a team-player who is accountable and responsible to others is another part of this skill. Showing up for sports practice, completing projects that are assigned, and doing one's part are all components of working with others and learning the importance of responsibility.

Helping others in the family, including younger siblings and even the household pet, are ways that children can contribute to the household and learn responsibility. Having the responsibility of feeding the family dog, helping a little brother, and reading to a younger sister all teach children that they are an important part of the family and have skills that are important to making everything work.

Doing their part for others and working together as a family are simple ways to teach responsibility at home. Learning that they play an important role in the household, no matter how small, can allow children to see how responsibility at home works.

By working together, both teachers and parents can help children learn responsibility. Through communication about a student's progress, homework concerns, and other child-oriented issues, adults can help children learn that responsibility is important in all areas of life.

## KEY IDEAS

- Responsibility is a skill that children need to learn at an early age as it will be needed for the rest of their lives.
- Responsibility starts in the home by completing simple chores and helping around the house.
- Teachers can also teach responsibility by creating a community environment in the classroom where everyone does his/her part.
- Homework and assignments are a great way to teach responsibility in the classroom.
- Having clear expectations, including penalties for being late, allows teachers to instruct students about responsibility.
- By working together, both parents and teachers can help teach the skill of responsibility to children.

# EIGHT

## Motivation

- Why is motivation important to children?
- How can educators teach motivation to children?
- How can parents teach motivation to children?

### IMPORTANCE OF MOTIVATION

Motivation is another soft skill that is important for children to learn. According to Gopalan et al. (2017): "The working definition of motivation is a persuasive feeling that always provides positivism to students to accomplish a task or activity to the end and succeed in it no matter how hard and tough it is."

Motivation applies to all areas of a child's life and includes motivation to accomplish a task at home, motivation to complete a project at school, and motivation to follow one's dreams—both in one's personal life and one's career. Teaching children the skill of motivation can be tricky as there is no set prescription or guide for how to do this.

Children often learn motivation by seeing someone who is inspirational, encouraging, and influential. It could be a parent or relative, a famous person, or a teacher. Regardless of the person who provides this motivation to children, learning to be positive, complete the tasks assigned, and be successful are all key. Even during hard times and roadblocks, students who learn the skill of motivation are those that persevere and reach goals, regardless of the barriers they face.

Motivation is often thought of as a skill that is practiced in schools and workplaces, as people complete courses, succeed in jobs, and complete goals. However, it also applies to one's home and personal life. Even young children can learn the skill of motivation as they persevere when building a tower of blocks, learn to read, and accomplish the skill of tying their shoes. Starting with these small tasks, both parents and teachers can encourage their determination, perseverance, and eventual success.

By encouraging, praising, and noticing even the small steps toward a child's accomplishments and setting goals that are both realistic and developmentally appropriate, both groups—parents and teachers—can help their children foster the soft skill of motivation. By encouraging small successes, learning to take baby steps, and working toward an attainable goal, adults can help children see that working hard and doing one's best will eventually pay off.

While the goal of motivation is to teach the child to learn *self-motivation*, learning this skill through the guidance of adults is the best way to start. Children do not arrive in the world being intrinsically motivated and knowing the steps needed to accomplish their goals. However, with the guidance of parents and teachers, they can learn how to persevere, work hard, and make goals happen.

Intrinsic motivation, or the idea that one achieves simply because one has the desire and will to do so without the need for rewards and praise, is the ultimate goal of motivation in children. While young children may need praise or a sticker for accomplishing a goal or returning their homework, they ultimately need to learn the skill of being intrinsically motivated to do their personal best in anything they choose to do.

While motivation may seem like a simple skill that all children need, teaching them to attain the intrinsic motivation that is necessary to succeed in adulthood is something that takes both time and effort from teachers and parents. The following section will tell how teachers can explain and model this skill in the classroom.

## HOW CAN EDUCATORS TEACH MOTIVATION TO CHILDREN?

Teachers are an influential part of learning motivation. Teachers who set high expectations, develop relationships with their students, and learn about students' strengths and interests are all things that can encourage their pupils in areas that excite and interest them. By motivating children to do their best, take risks in their learning, and set realistic goals, teachers can model that hard work and perseverance are an important skill for children.

Creating classroom environments in which children are allowed ownership of their learning encourages trying new things, allows for children to make mistakes, and enables teachers to promote motivation in their students' learning. Because motivation is one of the most important parts of engaging students in the classroom, this skill is important for all teachers to develop. The website Teach.com (2019) states that:

> One of the most difficult aspects of becoming a teacher is learning how to motivate your students. It is also one of the most important. Students who are not motivated will not learn effectively. They won't retain information, they won't participate, and some of them may even become disruptive.

By creating an environment of acceptance, encouraging students to do their best, and allowing students to pursue their interests and ambitions, teachers will motivate children to persevere and do their best in their learning.

Teachers can also motivate children to become involved in their learning by making lessons fun, interesting, and exciting. By doing hands-on activities instead of worksheets, allowing children to make choices in how they demonstrate their learning, and creating a fun atmosphere, teachers will model that learning is enjoyable and interesting. The effort put forth by a teacher to accomplish these goals is never wasted since children learn best when they are active and involved.

Encouragement and praise are also important factors in developing motivation in children. When teachers encourage students to do their best and are optimistic about doing well in their assignments, students are apt to do the same thing in their future. Teachers who are kind, reassuring, and positive will create students who are willing to take risks and are not afraid to make mistakes.

Helping children to set realistic goals, differentiating instruction to help children be successful, and creating materials that are interesting and motivating will help students realize their potential and learn the skill of motivation. Doing boring, dull, uninteresting activities will not promote enthusiasm for learning and can actually hinder the development of motivation in children. Teachers who create fun learning opportunities are more likely to develop learners who are motivated and excited to learn.

Teachers also need to learn when to ask for help from others when a student is deemed as being unmotivated. Talking to parents to find out about challenges the child might be facing, allowing parents to suggest ideas that might help or encourage learning, and working with others, such as the school counselor, can help teachers determine why motivation might be lacking and to find ways to encourage even the most unmotivated learner.

Knowing when to reach out for assistance, discovering ways that students learn best, and involving parents and families in the learning can all help teachers motivate learners and encourage families to contribute as well. Since parents are the child's first teacher, allowing parents to participate in their learning, offer suggestions that are motivating, and suggest ways that might help a teacher are all wonderful ideas for reaching unmotivated learners.

In conclusion, motivation is a skill that takes perseverance, dedication, and optimism to learn. Teachers who are encouraging, interesting, and allow students to take risks and make mistakes are those who children will remember as their coaches, cheerleaders, and influencers. By allowing students to explore their areas of interest, accommodating for various learning styles, and creating lessons that are interactive and fun, teachers can help students learn self-motivation and a love for learning that will last a lifetime.

Parents are vital to teaching about motivation too. By working together with teachers, they can help children learn about motivation as well. The following ideas can be used by parents to teach this soft skill in the home.

## HOW CAN PARENTS TEACH MOTIVATION TO CHILDREN?

Teaching children to be motivated is a skill that parents can begin at a very young age. When a parent encourages a child to take their first steps, pick up the toys after playing with them, and get dressed with no assistance, they are teaching their children to work hard and accomplish their goals. Even though these items may seem trivial, children learn at a young age that if they do things on their own, people notice.

Noticing and praising children for their accomplishments is one of the most important things parents can do to teach children the soft skill of motivation. When we have parents coaching us to succeed, we want to do more to show them our accomplishments. Children of all ages work harder when they are encouraged, motivated, and stimulated to do well.

While young children may need stickers for doing daily chores or accomplishing small tasks around the home, older students, eventually, need to be intrinsically motivated. In other words, children need to learn to do tasks simply because they are expectations for the family to be successful. Feeding the dog not because one gets a sticker but because it is one's family responsibility is an example of intrinsic motivation.

Doing chores because they are the right thing to do or working for good grades in school because one wants to be successful in life are both examples of intrinsic motivation. They are both important tasks, and both display a sense of maturity in children when they learn to work toward goals for personal fulfillment or responsibility and not simply for rewards and praise.

Learning personal satisfaction can go a long way in developing the skill of motivation in children. Renée Bacher, author of the article "6 Ways to Motivate your Children" (2019), states: "Encourage him to follow the lead of what makes him feel good inside—such as satisfaction in a newly learned skill or a job well done. He's not only more successful in the long term, he's also happy along the way, and inspired."

By teaching children to learn how to accomplish goals, learning satisfaction for a job well done, and being inspired simply by doing one's best, children will learn the beginning skills of motivation. These preliminary skills and the feeling of being successful create a beginning for the soft skill of motivation.

As children get older, learning to be motivated by their interests and strengths is another way that parents can encourage motivation in children. Children who love a specific hobby or want to play a musical instrument will learn motivation as they engage in a new skill, practice what they learned, and are successful in doing what they love to do.

Motivation in school is also an important factor for parents to encourage and stimulate. Parents who show an interest in school, help with homework, and are active in a child's education are modeling the importance of schoolwork in a child's life. Reading to a child, discussing what the child is learning, and taking an active interest in school are all simple and inexpensive ways that a parent can promote and encourage education at home.

Noticing when a child receives a good grade on a test, brings home a great report card, or even shows improvement in a subject that they have been struggling with are all ways that a parent can promote motivation and the importance of education in a child's life. When children receive praise and encouragement from their parents, they are more likely to do better in school and have a positive attitude toward learning.

Parents can model motivation, as well. When parents show their motivation in jobs, personal goals, and accomplishments, children will see this skill in action and are likely to follow this model as well. By sharing accomplishments from work, goals about personal interests, and ideas about how to reach these goals, children will see the value of working hard and being motivated to do well.

Overall, parents who encourage children to take risks, do their best, and achieve goals that are realistic in nature will motivate children to do well and reach their aspirations in life. Also, by communicating with educators, coaches, and adults in their children's lives, parents will show their children that they are committed and dedicated to helping their children succeed.

## KEY IDEAS

- Motivation is the idea of working hard and persevering, even if the task is difficult.
- Encouragement and praise are both ways to develop motivation in children.
- Parents can teach motivation by inspiring children to do their best and noticing even small accomplishments.
- Teaching the concept of intrinsic motivation is an important goal for children to learn.
- Teachers can model and encourage motivation in their classrooms, as well.
- Parents and teachers can work together to encourage children to succeed and do well in their endeavors.

# NINE
## Resilience

- Why is the skill of resilience important to children?
- How can educators teach the skill of resilience to children?
- How can parents teach the skill of resilience to children?

### IMPORTANCE OF RESILIENCE

Resilience is a soft skill that children need to succeed in today's world. According to Dictionary.com (2019), resilience is the "ability to recover readily from illness, depression, adversity, or the like." Resilience is being able to *bounce back* after bad things happen. It is remaining positive even through the rough times and having the *grit* to keep trying even after failure. Resilience means that kids may have an interruption or difficulty in their lives but can learn to continue with their lifestyle despite any adversity they encountered.

Kids today have a lot to deal with. They must do well in school, take care of family commitments, and participate in extracurricular activities. There is a great deal of pressure to succeed, whether that be by maintaining a certain grade point average, kicking the game-winning field goal, or earning badges in scouting activities. Many children put pressure on themselves to succeed, and parents and teachers often add to this load as well.

However, what happens when a major life event occurs, such as the death of a parent, a divorce in the family, or a mother who is deployed in the military? Children need to have the guidance and strength to be

51

successful, overcome obstacles, and have the support necessary to keep going with their daily lives.

Knowing the abilities and characteristics of children and being able to support them through the tough times is where resilience comes in. In stressful times, children will react differently. Some will become very quiet, some will need constant reassurance, and still others will just shut down. Being kind, nurturing, and compassionate to the child's needs is a key factor in helping them. If a child needs to cry, yell, or scream—let them. If a child needs to draw a quiet picture, self-soothe, and remain quiet—allow them to do so. In other words, allow children to grieve in their own way while providing support and a loving home or school environment in which to do so.

While major life changes such as death, divorce, or illness are often precursors to resilience, sometimes something as simple as a problem with friendships, a family move, or difficulty with schoolwork or a sports team can cause a child to need the skill of resilience. Even though these events may seem ordinary to adults, they can cause confusion, anxiety, and sleepless nights for children. Being aware of these problems as an adult can help one provide guidance and reassurance to a child who is struggling.

By teaching the skill of resilience to children, teachers and parents can help them learn coping skills, stress relief strategies, and survival skills— even when the world seems to be crumbling around them. Teachers and parents who model this skill themselves and have an optimistic outlook are the first part of teaching resilience to children. The next section will explain how educators can teach this skill in the classroom.

## HOW CAN EDUCATORS TEACH RESILIENCE TO CHILDREN?

Teachers can teach and model the skill of resilience in the classroom setting. By being aware of the normal behaviors and actions of students, a good teacher will be able to notice when a child is not behaving normally or seems upset about something. A quick conversation and a listening ear can help the teacher determine if a child needs help, if a parent contact might be needed, or if there is something in the classroom that is causing a child to be anxious or upset.

Having a good relationship with the school counselor or other experts at the school will enable a teacher to work collectively with others if a child experiences a traumatic experience, such as the illness of a parent. Also, encouraging parents to keep the teacher informed of changes in the schedule and lifestyle of children is a great way to keep the lines of communication open between school and home.

Teaching social skills such as problem-solving, anti-bullying strategies, and conflict resolution are also strategies that can be taught and implemented in the classroom. By giving students the *power of words*, teachers emphasize that communicating about problems and standing up for oneself and others is a valuable skill in today's world. Also, teaching students what to do if they have issues or problems with others is an important part of this strategy.

Surrounding students with positive posters and quotes such as Epictetus' "It's not what happens to you, but how you react to it that matters" is another way that teachers can reinforce the skill of resilience in the classroom. Creating an atmosphere of kindness, acceptance, and community will enable children to feel comfortable talking to others about problems they may be having and can create a support system as well. Sometimes just knowing that one is not alone can help children be more resilient in the face of adversity.

Doing stress-relief activities such as yoga for children, brain breaks, and other quick activities are ways that teachers can promote healthy lifestyles and teach children coping skills when they encounter stressful situations. While these strategies will not cure every stressful time in a child's life, having these tools will possibly enable minor problems to be de-escalated before they become larger.

Allowing children to have free time and a break when needed can also help children learn the skill of resiliency. When a child is dealing with a problem at home or school, simply allowing a *timeout* that is not accompanied by a consequence or penalty is a welcome idea for such students. An extra bathroom break, a walk in the hallway, or a quiet place in the classroom can all do wonders for getting a child back on track in the daily routine of the classroom. As long as children are not taking advantage of such situations, allowing these breaks can help them get away from the stressors—if even for a few minutes.

Reading about famous people who faced adversity and overcame obstacles is another way that children can learn about the skill of resiliency. Discussing the tools and approaches that the people used to overcome their problems is a way to model these same approaches to children.

Discussing and developing skills such as perseverance and determination are ones that can help children survive—both in third grade and in life!

Teachers who are aware of the normal behaviors of their students know when to intervene, and can create partnerships with parents and other school employees that can help children who are experiencing anxiety and stress in their lives. By being approachable, kind, and welcoming, children are more apt to tell teachers when something is bothering them.

Teaching relaxation skills, stress-relief strategies, and problem-solving strategies are also useful tools for teaching resilience. Finally, creating an environment of acceptance and learning about others who overcame obstacles can be useful in the classroom as well.

By communicating with parents and families, being willing to work with others, and offering support and encouragement when children are going through trying times, teachers can help teach the skill of resiliency in students. The world has many problems and stressors, even for the youngest children. Learning how to cope and work through them is a soft skill that children need in today's world. The next section will provide examples of how parents can help as well.

## HOW CAN PARENTS TEACH RESILIENCE TO CHILDREN?

Parents are often the first to notice stress and anxiety in children. They may not have the appetite that they used to, may have trouble sleeping, or show signs of sadness or depression. In the event of a major life change such as the death of a grandparent, an illness in the family, or an upcoming separation from a family member, parents are likely to know the cause of this stress and be able to provide reassurance, extra hugs, and nurturing to their kids.

However, not all stressors in life are as apparent to parents and caregivers. Sometimes, difficulty in school, a problem with peers, and anxiety about activities can also cause stress in children. There may not be one obvious trigger, but being in tune with a child's normal activities and behaviors can help a parent realize that something is wrong in a child's life.

In the *Handbook of Resilience in Children* (2014), Sam Goldstein and Robert Brooks state:

The concept of resilience is fairly straightforward if one accepts the possibility of developing an understanding of the means by which children thrive emotionally, behaviorally, academically, and interpersonally either in the face of risk and adversity or not.

Being open, approachable, and honest with children can help them identify the stressors and reasons that they may be feeling nervous or anxious. Helping them brainstorm a list of solutions and taking ownership of the problem can help them to learn coping skills, develop strategies, and implement new plans to help them be successful and alleviate the problems in their lives.

When children have adversity in their lives, even the smallest problem can develop into a big one. Helping children overcome this adversity, regardless of what the source of the problem is, can teach children to be resilient. Parents who take the time to listen and are willing to help children with their problems are those who can help them learn to cope with stress and overcome their problems.

At the same time, parents need to know when a simple talk or brainstorming session to come up with some problem-solving ideas are just not enough. A child who is having difficulty managing everyday activities and is stressed beyond what is normal for them may need professional help through a counselor, psychologist, or therapist who specializes in the needs of children. Starting with the family doctor is a great way to get recommendations and find resources for making this happen.

Acknowledging when a problem is beyond the extra support and reassurance of a parent or family member is not a sign of weakness. It simply means that another person may be more effective in helping the child to be resilient and learn to cope with their adversity. Asking for help from an additional person, such as a counselor or therapist, is also a great way for parents to model that one does not have to tackle their problems alone. Building a support system for the child and encouraging him/her to seek solutions with the help of others is an admirable trait in parents.

Communicating concerns and issues to teachers, involving a school counselor, and requesting support from the school and community are also ways that parents can get the help they need when their child is exhibiting signs of trauma or anxiety. Keeping teachers informed when a parent or grandparent is ill, sharing the news of an expected new sibling, or simply letting others know about changes in a child's life will alert adults to keep an extra eye on the student and be prepared for any sudden disruptions in the behavior and normal routines of children.

By working together as a team, parents and teachers can help a child by being on the same page, communicating the same plans for assistance, and exercising consistent expectations. Guiding children through both everyday issues and major problems in life will help them learn to persevere and learn the skill of resilience. By learning this skill at an early age, children will be better prepared for both college and career-related experiences that they will encounter in the future.

## KEY IDEAS

- Resilience is the idea that children can recover from problems and adversity.
- Adversity can come in the form of major life changes such as illness, death of a family member, and divorce. However, it can also be in the form of smaller stressors such as schoolwork and friendship issues.
- Teachers can help teach resilience by modeling and teaching coping strategies in the classroom.
- Parents need to be aware of changes in their child and be willing to accept help if needed.
- Parents and teachers need to communicate and create a team plan for helping children who are experiencing stress and anxiety.
- Resilience is a soft skill that children will use forever and a skill that will help them be successful in all areas of their lives.

# TEN

## Integrity

- Why is integrity an important skill for children?
- How can educators teach the skill of integrity to children?
- How can parents teach the skill of integrity to children?

### IMPORTANCE OF INTEGRITY

The famous author C. S. Lewis once said: "Integrity is doing the right thing even when no one is watching" (Lewis, no date). Integrity includes items such as honesty, values, and compassion. It means teaching a child to be ethical, make good choices, and practice sincerity. Integrity also involves putting yourself in someone else's shoes and thinking about how one would feel in a similar situation. The skill of integrity is one that children learn by being around good people who model good choices in their everyday lives.

Integrity is modeling one's beliefs and values and making decisions that accompany these values. It is not just talking about being a good and honest person; it is about making the choices that *show* one is a good and honest person. It is about establishing a system of beliefs and ethics and living them in one's daily life.

Children learn integrity through the examples of their caregivers and by being placed in difficult situations in which they must make decisions that will impact others. Learning the ideas of empathy and compassion can accompany the skill of integrity, as one's choices impact everyone around them. Knowing that *actions speak louder than words* and do not just impact one person are lessons that children need to learn at an early age.

Integrity also includes being a good person, even in the absence of parents and teachers. It is about making the right choices with a group of friends, finding money on the floor and turning it in, or helping someone without being told. Integrity is when children do the right thing without thinking about rewards and praise but simply because it is the moral thing to do.

Teachers, parents, and any adult in a child's life can model and teach the skill of integrity. Although some families may choose to develop this skill in a faith-based setting such as a church or synagogue, integrity can also be learned in everyday life. When a child makes a poor decision or makes an ill-advised choice, adults can help guide the child to a better option and can emphasize the importance of this choice as it impacts the child and others.

Teaching integrity is done by adults who model the skill themselves by being kind and moral people. They show children integrity simply by being good people and making proper choices in their daily lives. They also help children learn from difficult situations and guide them to make better choices after a misbehavior.

By helping children learn the soft skill of integrity, teachers and parents will raise children who make good choices, do the right thing, and are ethical citizens. Learning integrity helps children learn about the norms and rules of society while developing into good and just human beings as well. The following section will explain ways that integrity can be taught in the classroom.

## HOW CAN EDUCATORS TEACH INTEGRITY TO CHILDREN?

Teachers can show and model the soft skill of integrity in their classrooms. By displaying kindness and compassion to others, modeling correct behaviors for children, and guiding students in their decision-making and choices, teachers can show students the proper actions and alternatives for a school setting. Setting a good example for the children in one's classroom models both respect and integrity in the teaching profession.

Teachers are an important part of this soft skill because they are constantly modeling and being viewed by the children in the classroom. If they see their teacher doing the right thing, they are more apt to make such choices as well. For example, teachers who choose to follow the school rules such as not chewing gum in the classroom are showing children that they respect and abide by these rules and that such rules don't only apply to kids but all people in the school.

Modeling the skill of integrity is also done on a daily basis in the way that teachers treat and value the children in their classrooms. Treating each child with kindness, respecting all students, and avoiding favoritism are all actions that students notice. Doing one's best to be reasonable and unbiased—and being able to explain one's actions in special circumstances—are important for teachers to do in their classrooms.

Along with these actions are the ideas of fairness and consistency in the classroom. In an article in *Psychology Today* (2015), Marilyn Price-Mitchell states: "While teachers cannot control student behavior, they can respond with *consistency* when enforcing school and classroom policies. In a classroom culture that places learning first, dishonest behavior is a teachable moment."

Dealing with inappropriate behaviors in the classroom is a way that a teacher can use teachable moments and help children to learn better choices the next time a person is in the same predicament. Mistakes and poor choices happen in classrooms; from pre–K through college, however, how a teacher handles these circumstances is key. Helping children learn why an action was wrong, how it impacted others, and how to make a better decision in the future are all ways that a teacher can aide in the teaching of integrity.

Teaching social skills such as decision-making, honesty, and compassion are also strategies that teachers can use in the classroom. Noticing when a child makes a good decision or does the right thing is a wonderful way to begin this process in the classroom. When a teacher notices proper behavior in the classroom, it tends to have a *ripple effect* and will be noticed and copied by others in the classroom.

Reading about literary characters or talking about real people who have shown acts of integrity are also strategies for teaching this skill in the classroom. Many characters in books, both real and fictional, face choices in their lives. Reading and discussing these choices with children are tools for creating an understanding of integrity in the classroom. Asking why the character chose to *do the right thing* can create a lesson about why integrity matters both in the classroom and in life.

Telling children about a story in the news, such as a person who finds a large sum of money and returns it to the owner, is another way to teach integrity to children. Discussing why returning the money instead of keeping it (even though it was really tempting) is the right choice is a great way to explain the importance of right and wrong and how one's actions impact others.

Playing games and doing activities, such as "What Would you Do?", where a teacher explains a situation and asks the students what they would do in certain situations, are more ways to teach and model integrity in the classroom. Scenarios such as catching a friend cheating on a test can be discussed by the teacher, and students can share answers and explanations about what they would do in the same situation and why. Asking guiding questions and allowing the students to discuss in a nonjudgmental environment can help guide children in this process.

Overall, the soft skill of integrity is one that is needed in all aspects of life. Being a kind and moral person, making good decisions and ethical choices, and being fair to others are all characteristics that will help children be successful in life. By learning about integrity in academic settings, children will be able to carry this skill with them into their future. However, by involving parents, this skill can be emphasized even more.

## HOW CAN PARENTS TEACH INTEGRITY TO CHILDREN?

Parents begin teaching integrity from the time children are little by simply being good people themselves. Such parents model proper ethical behaviors, make good choices, and consider the feelings of others when they make decisions. They do the right things without considering rewards or recognition and consider how their actions impact the lives of others.

Parents can create homes with integrity by having a set of rules and guidelines for their children. Such homes have curfews and check-ins, monitor the use of electronic devices such as the television and video games, and allow children privileges that are based on age and maturity. As children show maturity and good choices in their lives, they earn more opportunities and privileges.

By not simply allowing children to do what they want and gradually releasing privileges as they earn them, parents are modeling that children who make proper choices are allowed to do more mature and exciting things. This part of integrity is one that varies between households, but it is a great way for children to learn that by making the right choices, they can earn even greater privileges.

Parents can teach integrity by having difficult conversations with their children. When friends are allowed to stay up without set bedtimes, play inappropriate video games, and do behaviors that are not acceptable in other families, children will often use the phrase, "But so-and-so is allowed to do it!"

By having conversations about why some behaviors are not allowed in their homes and why some activities are not acceptable to their parents, children will begin developing the moral background that they need to have in place to become compassionate adults who make good decisions. Sometimes explaining that all families do not make the same choices for their children is a good way to explain differences in parenting and belief systems. Remembering to not place blame on parents who make other decisions but simply saying that their parents love their children and want them to be good people is a nice way to explain this to children—though it's a conversation that may need to be repeated several times!

Having conversations about people in the news or situations in which children make inappropriate choices is another way to teach integrity to children. Talking about what the people did wrong and how they could have made better choices the next time exhibit a way to teach good decision-making skills in children. Emphasizing the idea of *learning from one's mistakes* can be a valuable tool for parents to use in such conversations.

As children get older, they will even bring situations of poor choices to the dinner table. School-age children like to report about the bad choices of others to their parents, tell about things that were done, and kids who got *in trouble.* Being able to debrief about such incidents and talk about ways the children could have made better choices can foster and teach the skill of integrity by using real-world examples.

Teenagers often point out students who are in trouble at school as well. Telling parents about situations such as other students who are expelled and in trouble with the law are often signs that they need approval and acknowledgment for not being in the same situation. Appreciating and valuing the proper choices of one's own children is another way that parents can confirm that their children are making the correct choices and actions.

Sometimes just being available to listen to the children in our lives is a way that adults can help children learn the skill of integrity. Having a willing listener who will help guide children to proper decisions and choices is one of the best ways that children can learn right from wrong. They often know the right choices but simply need the validation and respect from adults to do so.

Integrity is a skill that children learn by watching those around them. They gain this skill by watching their parents and families and by observing the values and ethics in their homes and those of their peers. Children learn integrity by talking about their choices and those of people they see in the news. They also learn integrity by making choices—some good and some bad. However, it is what they learn from those choices that can help children grow in the skill of integrity.

## KEY IDEAS

- Integrity means making the right choices, even when no one is watching.
- Integrity is teaching children to do the right thing in difficult situations.
- Teachers can model integrity by displaying consistency and fairness in their classrooms.
- Teachers can also instruct about integrity by using teachable moments, real-life situations, and characters in books who make good decisions.
- Parents can teach integrity by modeling ethical behaviors and talking about the choices that people make in their lives.
- By working together, both parents and educators can help teach this skill to children.

# ELEVEN

## Organization

- Why is the skill of organization important to children?
- How can educators teach organizational skills to children?
- How can parents teach organizational skills to children?

### IMPORTANCE OF ORGANIZATION

Organization is a skill that all people, regardless of age, need to have. Organization helps one feel safe, prepared, and ready for the day ahead. It implies that you care about your studies or your job, and it helps you stand out in the classroom and career world. Organization is often not noticed—until it is lacking.

Students who are lacking in organizational skills are those who can't find assignments, have messy desks, and often forget due dates and appointments. They sometimes misplace their backpacks, owe overdue fees at the library for lost books, and often look disheveled. Amanda Morin of Understood.Org (2019), an advocacy group for children with attention and learning needs, states the following:

> Kids who have weak organization skills struggle with handling information in an effective and logical way. They often have difficulty setting priorities, making plans, sticking to a task, and getting things done. These skills become increasingly important as your child moves through different grade levels.

Organization is a skill that can be taught and nurtured in the K-12 classroom and is important for parents and teachers to work on together. By teaching children organization, they will be more successful in school, will stick to projects and tasks, and will likely get better grades. It is hard to turn in assignments that are lost and forgotten.

While parents and teachers are often frustrated with children who lack organizational skills, there is hope for teaching this skill to children. Organization takes some time and a few supplies, such as calendars, labels, and notebooks, to achieve. However, the time and money invested in teaching children to be organized are well worth the effort.

Sometimes parents and teachers say that "organization is just not their thing" or "I'm not organized, but I get to work every day." While this may be true, the more organized their children become, the more successful those children will be in school. Preparing students for the skills and expectations of the school day and making sure children are ready with materials and assignments can make the school day go smoother for the students and is far less stressful than spending the day looking for things.

Teaching organization skills may seem like a minor problem for some children; however, this skill is vital to a student's success—both in the classroom and in their future at college and in careers. Children who learn organization skills at an early age will be more successful in learning and in life.

Educators play an important role in teaching the skill of organization to children. From the time children are little, they can begin to see that toys have their place, a routine happens each day, and things go better when the teacher is on time and organized in the morning! The following section will explain how teachers can teach the soft skill of organization to children.

## HOW CAN EDUCATORS TEACH ORGANIZATIONAL SKILLS TO CHILDREN?

Teachers who are organized are far more likely to produce students who are also organized. By modeling organization in the classroom, teachers can show the importance of taking care of school materials, following school routines, and having a place for everything in the classroom. All of these skills are easy to complete and cost very little to achieve in the classroom.

First, teachers need to be organized with materials in their classroom. By labeling homework trays, having a place to return materials, and teaching students to organize their own items, teachers will reinforce the importance of organization in the classroom. Also, little things like having all students write their names on papers and writing tasks in assignment notebooks can be helpful for both the organization of the teacher and the students.

Displaying a daily schedule of activities and assignments on the board or in a specific area is another great way to teach the skill of organization to children. Children will not only know the daily routine but will also see that teachers value the time spent in the classroom. By following a daily schedule as closely as possible, students will see that the teacher is organized and realize that time management is important for the skill of organization.

Allowing students to create learning contracts and complete projects is another way to teach organization in the classroom. Having older students create schedules and goals for learning, will create a path for learning and see how organization is an important life skill as well. When students enter college, they typically receive a syllabus for the semester, and knowing how to plan and work ahead will be a helpful skill to know before they arrive at their college of choice.

Teachers can also encourage planning skills by helping students with personal organization such as writing down tasks in an assignment notebook or adding them to a calendar app on their smartphones. In addition, some students may need some extra assistance, such as writing down materials that are needed the next day or remembering an important school event. By helping students with this visual plan, teachers will show why organization is a vital skill in their lives.

Finally, modeling by thinking aloud is a great skill for teachers to use with their students. Planning a project or sharing about one's plans for the month are ways that teachers can model the skill of organization in their classrooms. Allowing students input into the real world of adults shows the students that organization is an important skill for all ages.

Overall, learning the soft skill of organization is an attribute that all people can benefit from. If teachers and parents work together, they can help children be prepared with materials, assignments, and other items that will help students be productive, and they will model the importance of organization in the real world.

Parents and teachers who help children with schedules and outside activities are also teaching the importance of the organization process.

The following will explain some ideas that parents can use to teach organization in the home.

## HOW CAN PARENTS TEACH ORGANIZATIONAL SKILLS TO CHILDREN?

Children begin learning organization skills far before they enter the classroom. They feel a sense of *normalcy* when things are running smoothly in their homes. They know what it is like on a regular morning versus a hurried one. While many parents know that a home should be clean and organized, they often don't realize how organization helps their children in other ways.

Morin of Understood.org (2019) states:

> If your child has organization issues, opening her backpack can be a frightening experience. Crumpled assignments and tests, school announcements from two months ago, her missing house key—it's a mess! Many people think of organization skills as the ability to keep things in order. But people also use those skills to keep their thoughts in order so they can retrieve information and use it effectively.

As stated above, organization is much more than just the papers in a desk or backpack. Organization includes one's thoughts and actions as well. It is about being prepared for the day and having an organized mindset. While it can be frustrating to parents, the skill of organization for children is indeed important to their success. Developing these skills at an early age will follow children into adulthood and beyond. The following are ways that parents and families can help teach these skills at home.

To be organized, a child needs first to understand the importance of this skill. Expecting a kindergarten child to be organized on her own is most likely unattainable. Instead, parents need to explain that organization means knowing where your materials are, being prepared and ready for school each day, bringing home communication such as school notes and announcements, and being mentally organized.

Parents can teach organization by having a routine in place as much as possible. If children get home from school, have a snack, and get homework done before other activities, they can then put homework in their backpacks and be ready for the next day. Of course, this routine will not work every night, but sticking to it as much as possible will instill a sense of organization in children.

Practicing the motto "a place for everything, and everything in its place" is also a great way to teach organization. If one teaches the skill of putting things back after they are used, children will be more likely to do so in the future. When toys are played with, putting them back in toy boxes or labeled crates will be helpful in not only teaching the skill but also finding things the next time they are needed. When the scissors and school supplies are used, they need to go back in the drawer. Insisting on routine with materials works well with young students, but indeed, it may take some effort with teenagers!

Having a family calendar posted in a prominent place in the kitchen or family room is also helpful in teaching organization. As each member of the family receives schedules and dates, they can add to the family calendar. Encouraging children to be responsible for adding their own activities, such as soccer practice, scouts, science fairs, and religious events, can help them be organized in time and activities as well.

Older students with computers and cell phones can add activities to their calendars and notes sections to remind them of dates and plans for the future. Since this skill will be beneficial in college and careers, learning it as middle and high school students is helpful. Knowing how to organize activities and due dates is a great skill to have in the future. Any parent who has remembered soccer practice 20 minutes before they were to get children to the soccer field will also appreciate this effort by their families.

Parents can also teach organization by modeling it themselves. Thinking aloud about what they need to do tomorrow at work, writing lists for the grocery store, and planning carpool for the upcoming week show children how organization is helpful to adults as well. Even better, having children help with the grocery lists and activity planning are important life skills that they can use in the future. Children can help check for milk in the refrigerator, write the lists for the store, and help restock cabinets after the shopping is done. By doing activities that show organization, children will learn why the skill is vital, and in turn, they will help their family as well.

Another activity that can help children with organization is laying one's clothes, backpacks, sports gear, and other needed items out the night before. Looking for the other shoe in the morning can mean missing the school bus and arriving late to school, adding stress for both parents and children. However, if the clothes and supplies are laid out in the same place before going to bed, the idea of a calm morning is attainable.

In all, parents who model organization, follow through with clean up each night, and teach children to help with planning for activities and other family functions not only shows the importance of this soft skill, but it can also save time and energy for tired parents. Although it may take some time and effort in the beginning, if children are taught routines at an early age, they are far more likely to have these skills in place when they enter their first classrooms.

## KEY IDEAS

- Organization skills are needed by people of all ages.
- Children who lack organizational skills often lose assignments and forget due dates.
- Organizational skills directly impact one's success in the classroom.
- Organization is a soft skill that can be taught and nurtured.
- Parents and teachers should work together to practice organizational skills that will help children in their learning.
- Children who learn organizational skills at an early age will take this soft skill into their future college and career options.

# TWELVE

# Time Management

- Why is time management an important skill for children?
- How can educators teach the skill of time management to children?
- How can parents teach the skill of time management to children?

## IMPORTANCE OF TIME MANAGEMENT

Time management is a soft skill that can be used by children as well as adults. Being on time for classes and meetings, being aware of time and space, and using time in a productive manner are all important for children to learn. Time management also impacts one's ability to organize and prioritize items that must be done daily.

In a recent edition of *Psychology Today*, Eileen Kennedy-Moore (2014) stated, "Understanding time helps kids to use their time well. It's a key part of executive functioning skills such as planning and prioritizing."

Being aware of time and how it works is a basic skill that all children need. From the time a child is little, being aware of schedules such as breakfast in the morning, lunch at midday, and dinner in the evening are some of the first time-oriented events that children learn. Also, the sequencing of events in the day helps children learn that routine can be a helpful way to stay organized and on top of things.

Time management is especially helpful as children reach school age and begin to learn that *there is only so much time in a day.* By learning to use time and schedules effectively, school-age children will be able to develop the skill of time management that they will use for the rest of their lives. Regardless of the career path that one eventually chooses, being on time and using this valuable resource efficiently will help children be better prepared for the future.

Time management helps with organization, planning, scheduling, and many other elements that help both children and adults. Being able to manage one's time can help prepare students for the future and will enable them to see the importance of making the most of every minute of their day.

There are many ways that both teachers and parents can help children learn the skill of time management. Being able to create and follow schedules, work under time demands, and use time efficiently are all ways that adults can help children learn this skill. The following are ways that teachers can teach and model this skill for children.

## HOW CAN EDUCATORS TEACH TIME MANAGEMENT TO CHILDREN?

Teachers are important in teaching and modeling the skill of time management for children. In most elementary schools, a schedule of subjects, lunch, and recess are all dictated by the administration. Teachers who follow these schedules model the soft skill of time management to their students. If they are prompt and on time, the students will see the importance of following schedules, and the other school faculty who are involved (such as cafeteria workers and special-area teachers) will appreciate that their schedules are not hindered by the tardiness of others.

Students in junior high and high school are often penalized for arriving *after the bell*, so learning time management at an early age will help them as well. Teachers in the upper grades who follow bell schedules and begin each new class promptly model that their teaching time is important and that the learning time of students is valued.

Teachers can also model time management by creating a homework schedule. Having certain items done on a routine schedule can help both parents and children plan for the assignments that are expected each week. Providing a schedule to parents that is consistent and familiar can help families plan for the week and ensure that homework is completed each evening. For example, if students study math facts on Mondays, do reading on Tuesdays, and so on, parents will know what to expect and can help their children plan their time accordingly.

For older students, assigning a project that is done in stages and has a calendar for completion can help students learn time management. If a completed project is due in two weeks, giving the students checkpoints along the way will benefit students who tend to procrastinate. Having the project outline due on Day 2, a model due on Day 4, and steps of the research outlined for the rest of the project will help children learn to manage their time and will help teachers stay organized as well.

As students prepare for high school and college, teaching them about scheduling and study time is also a useful life skill. Teaching students how to read and use a class syllabus, plan for projects and assignments, and create a dedicated study time are all useful to students but are rarely taught as required study skills in today's classrooms. Teachers who take the time to do this will create students who understand the importance of schedules, timelines, and due dates, all tools that are needed for today's scholars.

Creating a homework folder, assignment notebook, and family communication plan can also help teachers instruct students about time management. Oftentimes, something visual such as a calendar or checklist can help children see what is due, what is completed, and what still needs to be finished. Sending this information home on a daily or weekly basis also creates a routine that both children and parents appreciate. Teachers who hand out random assignments, expect projects finished that are not given the ample time to complete, and do not provide feedback in an appropriate amount of time can cause stress for students.

By creating homework folders and assignment notebooks, children can practice time management and learn this skill at a very young age. Older students who use class calendars and syllabi will practice using the time management that will be needed for both college and career readiness.

On a final note, teaching children that sometimes taking a break from schoolwork is also important. Just like adults who have coffee breaks, lunch schedules, and a short time for relaxing between activities, children need the same unscheduled time in their day. When teachers notice that children are bored or overwhelmed with the content of a lesson, taking a *brain break* can be very effective. According to UNICEF (2019):

> Brain Breaks for kids is the simple technique in which young students are given a short mental break taken at regular intervals. Most brain breaks range from around 5 to 20 minutes as a general rule, although

most people prefer to keep them short and on point. For maximum success, it's usually best to include a physical activity that will complement mental energy.

Brain breaks work for all children from preschool to high school age. Sometimes, simply taking a short break from academics can renew and refresh both the mind and the body and allow children time to redirect and refocus after a quick but valuable activity. Even though this takes a few minutes from the schedule, the productivity that follows a brain break can be remarkable.

One other break that will help children is the idea of recess. Recess, a time for unstructured play, allows students a break from academics and encourages free play and physical exercise. While many schools are decreasing or even eliminating recess from school schedules, researchers at Harvard Health (2015) found that "The loss of unstructured time for students may not be achieving its aims. Students who are kept in classrooms all day without a break are likely to be less attentive and may also learn less efficiently."

While teaching children to properly manage their time, learn organization of projects, and work within schedules in a school setting, learning to take the time just to relax and play is also an important part of time management. As adults know, taking a walk, having a coffee break, and stretching for a minute can help them get back on task; students need to learn that a quick break can benefit one's time on task as well.

In conclusion, teachers play an important role in teaching children about time management. By teaching the importance of following schedules, using planning strategies, and helping with routines and schedules, educators can help children with this important skill. On the same note, teaching children to take breaks and refocus is also a vital part of learning time management in the classroom.

Parents can help with time management as well. By working together with teachers, they can help children learn this important skill. Being able to manage one's time, arrive on time for appointments and work-related activities, and other tasks are all indeed skills needed to be college and career ready. The following section will explain how parents can help with this skill at home.

# HOW CAN PARENTS TEACH TIME MANAGEMENT TO CHILDREN?

Parents are busy people. There are jobs to do, chores to attend to, and dinner to prepare. Keeping the family in a routine and schedule are often hard to do, with so much going on both in and out of the home. However, parents who model the skill of time management and teach children about being prepared and ready will raise children who do the same.

Very early in a child's life, he/she can begin learning about time management. Beginning with concepts such as morning and evening, or wake up and night time, children can learn that very specific things happen during these hours. Developing a schedule that one follows in the morning and at bedtime are ways that a young child can learn about using time efficiently and teaches the concept of sequencing as well. Doing a routine each night that includes brushing teeth, getting a drink, and reading a story is a great way to begin teaching time management to young children.

As children get older, creating a schedule, either in pictures or words, can help them put their mornings together. Some parents even create a checklist that helps children remember the steps of getting ready for school. Those who have children who are not *morning people* may find this especially helpful in getting out the door in the mornings!

Time management for routines, laying out clothes for the next morning, having lunches packed and in the refrigerator, and backpacks ready to go can all help the morning routines go smoother and quicker. By teaching about the elements of routine and organization, children can learn that by being organized and ready, they will also have more time to get things done.

Homework is often a stressful topic for families. However, creating a routine for homework can also be helpful to school-age children. Allowing children a few minutes of *downtime* to just decompress and relax, perhaps followed by a healthy snack, is a great way to ease into the homework challenge. Then, after a set time (usually an hour or less), children should begin homework and get it finished before being allowed video games, television, or electronic time. By having a set homework schedule each afternoon/evening, children are more apt to complete homework and are less likely to be stressed about its completion.

For older children, keeping a homework notebook that is written in each day is a very helpful tool for both home and school. As children complete the homework each evening, they can check off the items and know that the items are finished and ready to turn in the next morning. For busy children who know ahead of time that they have a soccer game during the week, encouraging them to work ahead on projects and assignments can also help alleviate last-minute stress and anxiety—for both children and parents.

Creating a schedule, both for the individual child and the family, can also help with the soft skill of time management. Some families create a color-coded calendar in which all of the family events are planned and coordinated. With each member of the family receiving their own unique color, it is easy to see at a glance the schedule for the week. By displaying a calendar on the refrigerator or a common area in the house, parents can model how to plan for the week, and children can see where they spend the majority of their time.

Parents who see that their children are overscheduled and stressed can also point out how many activities a child is doing and suggest that maybe they cut down on certain activities or reallocate their time. While this may not be easy to do simply through conversation, sometimes a visual of the week can represent just where time is being spent. Prioritizing events and activities by importance and interest can help children use their time more wisely and effectively.

In brief, learning the skill of time management is a tool that can help children far into the future. Time management is not just used by young children; it also helps as college students begin managing course schedules and adult workers complete projects in a timely manner. Learning this skill at an early age and teaching the importance of routine are ways that adults can be involved in this process.

KEY IDEAS

- Time management is a skill that begins with very young children as they learn a sense of time and routine.
- Teachers can help students learn time management skills by adhering to schedules and teaching about the impact of timeliness on learning.
- Teachers can also help students learn time management in the creation of homework schedules and project checkpoints.

- Parents can help children learn time management by creating schedules and routines in the mornings, for homework, and at bedtime.
- Creating family schedules can help with time management and help make activities less stressful.
- Learning time management, as well as when to take a break and refocus, are skills that children will use for a lifetime.

# THIRTEEN

## Balance

- Why is the skill of balance important to children?
- How can educators teach balance to children?
- How can parents teach balance to children?

### IMPORTANCE OF BALANCE

According to the Oxford Dictionary (2019), the word balance means "an even distribution of weight enabling someone or something to remain upright and steady; mental or emotional stability; the way to some kind of peace and personal balance." While one normally thinks of balance regarding standing on one foot without falling over, it also applies to having everything in one's life balanced.

Concerning children, balance means having activities, schoolwork, and other needs in place so that one does not lose control. It means that a child is involved and busy, without being overcommitted. Children who are balanced can participate in extracurricular activities, enjoy school, and have family time without feeling stressed or overwhelmed.

In the classic book *The Hurried Child* by David Elkind (1981), the author pointed out that children are experiencing more stress than necessary and are being forced into the role of *miniature adults*. By adding pressure and stress to the lives of children, they often do not learn to attain balance in their lives and relationships. The book was a pinnacle in pointing out the need for balance in children.

Another way that balance has been defined in the lives of children is through the "Sandwich Analogy." According to Len Stauffenger (2019), a mental sandwich for children should include "part work, part play, part serious thinking, and part restful enjoyment . . . Because of the breadth of those four pieces, all that your kids' lives include are in there. You will be able to instantly see what is out of balance."

The sandwich model is a great way of showing children how balance is important in their daily lives. If their entire day is consumed with school and homework or sports activities, with little time to do other things, they will likely become tired, overwhelmed, and even stressed. Teaching children the important aspects of balancing the time and activities in their lives is an important soft skill that will take them into adulthood.

For children today, many opportunities are present through school, sports leagues, faith-based organizations, and others. Encouraging them to participate and be active in such organizations is important to both social and emotional needs. However, how does one participate and be happy without becoming over-committed and overly stressed? The following section will address the soft skill of balance and how teachers can help develop the skill in children.

## HOW CAN EDUCATORS TEACH BALANCE TO CHILDREN?

Teachers and educators play an important role in the balance of children. Just like they balance the school day with just the right amount of active learning and quiet learning, a teacher can play a huge role in creating a balanced lifestyle for his/her students.

One of the first things that comes to mind when thinking of how schools are a part of a balanced child's life is that of homework. While homework can have the healthy benefits of having the child review and apply new curriculum, too much of it can be overwhelming. The National Education Association "Research Spotlight on Homework" (2019) states the following:

> The National PTA recommendations fall in line with general guidelines and suggest 10-20 minutes per night in the first grade, and an additional 10 minutes per grade level thereafter (e.g., 20 minutes for second grade, 120 minutes for twelfth). High school students may sometimes do more, depending on what classes they take.

Teachers who assign homework within these guidelines will model the idea that homework is important but also that this is not the only thing that children should be doing in the evening. Teachers who promote family activities, reading at bedtime, and playing outside will produce children who are well-rounded and not overwhelmed with hours of homework each night.

Another idea for teaching balance in the school day is by using this technique in lesson planning and curriculum for one's teaching. Creating a balance of project-based learning, with pencil and paper work, will help students see a balance in the school day. Also, doing different activities throughout the day, such as a balance of group and individual work, will also teach and model that children learn in a variety of ways and that different approaches will help reach the needs of all students in the classroom.

For older students, the idea of contracts or syllabi is helpful in creating balanced students. When introducing a new project, for example, a teacher can model an appropriate timeline for completing the daily activities that lead up to the final product. By modeling how to pace one's learning, complete projects in small *chunks,* and planning for each part on a daily basis, teachers can show children how to balance their time and energy in the school setting. Creating a contract for learning, with an estimated timeline for each step of the project, is a visual way for students to see their progress as well as what still needs to be completed.

Homework binders or home/school communication folders are also a great way to share information with parents and families. By having a communication system in place with homework for the week and announcements about school activities and other events, parents will be able to help children balance their home and work lives.

For older students, a syllabus for the class with due dates, projects, and tests on it will help them balance their school and home lives. If a child has a family function, teaching them to work ahead can benefit them regarding time management and stress reduction. This is also a great skill for students to have as they approach college and career readiness, as a balanced workload will prevent cramming for tests, having all-night study sessions, and panicking at the last minute when projects are not completed.

Working with a school counselor on presentations for students is another great way to build balance in children. School counselors or other mental health professionals can create short lessons on how to balance home and school, when activities are just too much, and how to prioritize the events in a child's life. Sharing examples of a child who is doing too much can be a great way to model this soft skill for children.

Finally, a teacher who shares about his/her own balancing act can have a huge impact on students. Thinking aloud with comments such as, "Wow. I have a lot on my plate this week, with all of those projects to grade and a baseball game for my son. However, I know that I can grade a bit each night and get all of it done," can show students that adults have to balance things as well. As long as the teacher is not complaining about the workload, sharing the idea of balance with children is important.

Also sharing how the teacher does things for fun can model the idea of balance in the classroom. Sharing a few personal stories, such as how the teacher participates in family events, a yoga class for relaxation, or a book club for outside reading, can model the idea of taking care of one-self outside the classroom and promotes a healthy view of a working adult who has a balanced life.

In conclusion, teachers can do a great deal to help children learn the soft skill of balance. By learning to have an even amount of outside activities, family time, schoolwork, and playtime, children will be able to attain balance in their lives. Working together to make sure that children are not overscheduled or overcommitted, teachers and parents can help develop the whole child, one who is happy and healthy instead of over-whelmed and stressed. The following section focuses on strategies that can be taught in the home.

## HOW CAN PARENTS TEACH BALANCE TO CHILDREN?

Many opportunities exist for children to be active and participate with friends in activities and adventures. Being able to be a part of a group or organization is important in the development of self-esteem and social skills. Children naturally want to explore new adventures, have fun with friends, and be active and busy. However, at what point do parents say that enough is enough?

The idea of balance in children is one that involves making sure that children have a healthy proportion of home, school, and outside activities while maintaining a level of harmony and happiness. It means that a child can be home for Sunday dinner with the family and keep homework and grades in check while still enjoying outside activities with friends.

Modeling balance by parents and caregivers is a great way to practice balance in the home. If children see parents who work every night, run from one activity to the next, and are overcommitted themselves, their kids are likely to model this as well. While leaving that stack of papers at work or calling a client from the office instead of the home may be challenging for parents, it is important that children see them having downtime as well.

Parents can help to achieve a balance in their children's lives in various ways. First, it is important to examine the personal family values and time constraints that exist in the lives of their children. One quick and easy way to determine this is by looking at the family calendar and deciding which activities are most important and which are the most time-consuming.

Designing a calendar that lists all of the activities of each person in the family can help show how busy or scheduled a child is in the household. If the child is scheduled for an event or activity every day of the week, parents should ask if this is too much and if the children have time to relax, do healthy outdoor activities, and simply have *downtime*.

Along with this is the idea of allowing time in the week where the children have no commitments, activities, or events to attend. Having unplanned *playtime* in the week is a great way to make sure that kids are unplugged, active, and able to just enjoy time with friends and family. Having a "Fun Friday" or a "Sibling Saturday" allows children to interact with others without having to be at a prearranged activity.

Limiting activities to just one sport, one faith-based activity, and one school or club activity is another great way to achieve balance. While students may want to participate in every activity and sport that a school offers, learning to make choices and prioritize time commitments can lead to a more balanced lifestyle for children. Doing just one sport per season, one activity at school, and one outside activity, children will see that these commitments take time, energy, and devotion to make them all work.

Considering the age and developmental level of the child is also important in these choices. Younger children may need to start with just one activity and grow into others as they are more responsible and better at managing time. Parents will know when to add on these activities by watching how committed and interested their children are in doing them.

Another idea of the balance of activities and commitments for children has to do with interest and enjoyment. Oftentimes, children *think* they would like to try a new sport or club yet find out rather quickly that it isn't for them. Having a family rule that children must finish what they start is a great way for children to learn the idea of commitment to a team or a project. Finishing the baseball season, for example, shows that one is a good teammate and a dedicated person. Not signing up for the *next* season, however, is always an option!

Finally, parents need to step back and take a look at the reasons their children are involved in the activities and commitments that they are. Does she truly enjoy dance class? Does he cry at every soccer practice? On the ride home, does the child share the awesome things that happened in the club or complain about what happened or threaten to quit? Watching and listening to children is a great way to know if the children are indeed interested and willing, or simply going through the motions of the activity involved.

Parents have a lot on their plates, and balancing a family schedule can take a great deal of planning and execution. However, making sure that children have time for family, schoolwork, play, and rest is an important part of the development of children. Learning to prioritize, looking at the daily schedule, and having time just to be kids is an important part of being a child today. By working together, teachers and parents can help children learn this skill and be prepared to use this in their future educational and career endeavors.

## KEY POINTS

- Balance is the idea of planning one's activities and responsibilities in a way that is not overwhelming to children.
- Teachers can help with balance in the classroom by arranging content and curriculum appropriately.
- Teachers can also help with balance by providing appropriate homework that is respectful but not overwhelming.
- Balance includes unplanned time and downtime for children as well as families.

- Parents can help children learn balance by examining and prioritizing activities and creating a calendar as a visualization of these items.
- Learning the skill of balance will help prepare children for both college and career experiences.

# FOURTEEN

## Positive Attitude

- Why is a positive attitude important to children?
- How can educators teach about a positive attitude to children?
- How can parents teach about a positive attitude to children?

### IMPORTANCE OF POSITIVE ATTITUDE

A positive attitude is one of the most important things we can teach our children. Learning to look for the best in life, turning a bad day into a good one, and having a great outlook on life can help children be successful both in school and in the future. People who are negative and only look for the bad are often stressed, overwhelmed, and prone to more illness. Negative attitudes can impact everything that one does and can create environments of negativity in all areas of one's life.

A positive attitude, on the other hand, can promote positivity, wellness, and a healthy outlook. Being positive is an attribute that helps in the home, school, and office setting. It is a skill that children need to be successful, both in school and in future careers. Employers appreciate a positive attitude in the workplace, and people generally like to be around those with a positive attitude more than a negative one.

Teaching children to be positive is a soft skill that parents and educators can both teach and model for the children around them. By creating positive environments, having an optimistic outlook, and looking for the best in life, they show children from very early stages that a positive outlook can take you far. Parents and teachers who show children how to take a bad day and make it better are able to model for children that one bad incident in the day does not have to ruin it.

In today's world, children are facing more pressure, stress, and life changes than ever before. Learning to be hopeful and positive can help make life more manageable and is a skill that can be used forever. According to Ripa Ajmera of LiveStrong.com (2019):

> In a world filled with negativity, violence, and suffering, a positive attitude can make life more manageable. Although it's impossible to fully control life events, you can control your reactions to what happens. This attitude enables you to develop the strength to deal with life's challenges. When children develop a positive attitude early in life, positive thinking becomes a habit that can ease the pressures associated with growing up.

The power of *positive thinking* can be taught in many different ways, both at school and at home. By practicing a few simple things each day, both teachers and parents can teach this soft skill to children. The next section will explain how teachers can teach and model this skill in the classroom.

## HOW CAN EDUCATORS TEACH ABOUT A POSITIVE ATTITUDE TO CHILDREN?

There are a variety of ways that educators can teach and model a positive attitude in the classroom. The first begins with a positive outlook and nurturing environment. A teacher who is kind and welcoming every day, leaves personal problems at home, and creates a classroom that is community-oriented is modeling a positive outlook to the class. Even though changes in the schedule happen, a child acts out, or a bad thing happens, teachers need to remain positive to the best of their abilities.

Beginning each day as a new day—regardless of what happened in the past—is a great way to model positivity in the classroom. Teachers who hold grudges, bring personal problems into the classroom, or model negative behavior are likely to create students who act the same. Children look up to teachers and watch as they handle both the good and bad things that happen during the day. Teachers who can work through the negative are modeling this disposition to the children in their classroom.

Teachers can also create positive classroom environments by teaching about an affirming mindset in the classroom. A positive or growth mindset implies that the intelligence and outlook of children can be encouraged through attitude and effort in the classroom. Teachers who instruct children about the importance of believing in themselves, putting forth effort in the classroom, and working toward accomplishments can assist students in learning how to be positive. Recent research by the Education Week Research Center (2016) indicated the following:

> Teachers overwhelmingly agree that incorporating growth mindset into their practice could have significant effects for student learning and the quality of instruction. Nearly all of the teachers surveyed (98 percent) agreed that integrating the concept of students' growth mindset into their classroom practice will improve student learning (p. 26).

Along with a growth mindset in the classroom, teachers can also help with positive attitudes by having children set attainable goals and encouraging them to be successful. Teachers who allow children to set goals, help them achieve, and celebrate their successes will enable children to grow and learn about the idea of being positive. When children see that they can learn and achieve their goals, they are apt to be more positive about the next obstacle before them.

Teachers can also assist students in developing a positive attitude by placing an emphasis on encouraging words and phrases in the classroom. Creating a positive class motto, decorating the classroom with children's work and successes, and providing positive quotes and posters is another great way to create positivity. Inspirational and encouraging quotes in the classroom surround children with the positive energy they need to succeed.

Quotabulary.com (2018), a website that contains encouraging passages and quotations, states the following:

> Words which spread hope and influence the process of thinking in a positive manner are required for the purpose of motivation and the healthy growth of kids. Positive and encouraging quotes for kids . . . should act as a source of positive energy and shape the mind of kids.

By creating a positive environment, sharing encouraging words, and displaying optimistic quotes, teachers will model the idea of positivity and will show this belief to students and anyone else who enters the classroom. Since a positive attitude can be contagious, seeing such displays around them will encourage students to share such a disposition with others.

Teachers can also promote the idea of positivity in the classroom by using praise and encouragement with students. While all children will not do well on assignments or tests, providing praise for what they did correctly and encouraging them to do better the next time can go a long way in the classroom. By providing positive feedback to students, teachers can model the value of working hard, trying one's best, and remaining positive about the next task that students must attempt.

"Community Circles" or "Morning Meetings" are also excellent ways of creating positivity in the classroom and setting the tone for the day. By assembling the students for a quick Morning Meeting to talk about events for the day, discussing concerns from the children, and establishing a positive rapport for learning, teachers will create an environment of caring and nurturing. Listening to children and allowing them input into issues of the school or classroom encourages students that they have the power to make changes and the ability to be heard.

Using bibliotherapy, or the idea of reading a book with a particular purpose, is another way that teachers can instruct about a positive attitude in the classroom. Reading about a character who has a problem, is in an adverse situation, or is feeling sad can all display to children how to learn from problems and turn them into something more positive. Sometimes, reading about a character with a similar problem can help children learn that they are not alone in what they are dealing with.

Talking about real-life people in the world who are inspirational and demonstrate a positive attitude is another way to teach about this skill in the classroom. There are people all around us who model a positive attitude, have overcome a difficult situation, or rise to the top—despite difficult circumstances. Talking about these people, whether they are in the local community or in the national news, is a beneficial way for students to see that a positive attitude can help one with even the most difficult of problems.

In summary, teachers need to model and teach the importance of a positive attitude in the classroom. By creating an environment that focuses on positivity, is student-oriented, and focuses on community, students will have a place where they can share problems, make mistakes, and learn to be positive in difficult situations. Using community circles, displaying positive quotes, and involving students in decision-making can also be useful in creating nurturing environments in which children will thrive. Regardless of the strategies the teacher uses, modeling the idea of a positive attitude is one of the most important ones they can choose.

Parents, too, are an important part of teaching about a positive attitude to children. The following section explores ideas for teaching and modeling this skill at home.

## HOW CAN PARENTS TEACH ABOUT A POSITIVE ATTITUDE TO CHILDREN?

A positive attitude begins in the home, from the minute a child arrives. It involves being nurturing and confident in communicating with children and keeping a great attitude toward life. A positive attitude means working through the bad things that happen and continuing to be positive despite them. Although raising children can be an incredibly difficult and stressful experience, it is also one of the greatest joys that parents can have.

Modeling positive parenting through positive discipline, teamwork, and an encouraging environment will help children maintain an upbeat attitude that will help them in all areas of their schooling and future careers. By beginning the process with a positive home environment, parents can model this for their children.

According to Nina Gallegos (2019) from The Center for Parenting Education, "You can start by encouraging positive thinking and by creating an environment that nurtures your children's beliefs in their abilities. Having that confidence enables them to take risks that will help them reach their potential." By believing in the abilities of children and providing encouragement and support for them, parents begin the journey of teaching a positive mindset to their families.

Modeling and talking about how parents work through tough times is a great way to show children how to create a positive environment in their own lives. All parents have rough days, whether it is at home when an appliance breaks, at work when one deals with a difficult co-worker, or with a problem on a work-related project. However, showing children that it's not *the end of the world* can make a huge difference.

Sharing what caused the problem and how one plans to deal with it is beneficial to both parents and children. By thinking through the problem and brainstorming solutions together, parents will not only be able to determine resolutions, but they will also model this skill for children.

Handling problems in a calm manner can show them that even the worst problems can be turned into positive situations.

Parents can also teach a positive attitude by helping children with their own problems or concerns. If a child is worried about a confrontation with a friend or an upcoming test, parents can help children develop some possible solutions, share stories about similar events when they were younger, and learn that a positive outlook can help more than anything. Sometimes, an empathetic listener and encourager is all that a child needs to come up with his/her own solutions. Hopefully, by doing this, children will learn to turn the problem into a positive outcome.

In brief, children need to see a positive attitude modeled by the people in their lives. If they wake up each morning to a grumpy environment, they are apt to model this in their own lives. Seeing and living in a home of positivity can make a huge impact on school and future successes. Even in the roughest moments, children need to see a positive end in sight, and parents and teachers can be the keys to making this happen.

## KEY IDEAS

- Children need positive environments both at home and at school.
- Providing encouragement and modeling a positive attitude is important for both parents and teachers to do.
- Teachers can help children learn positive attitudes by using a growth mindset and setting attainable goals with the students.
- "Morning Meetings" and "Community Circles" are great ways to set the tone for the day in the classroom and promote a positive classroom environment.
- Parents can assist children in developing a positive attitude by sharing their own problems and modeling how they were solved.
- Teaching and modeling the soft skill of a positive attitude are lifelong skills that all children need.

# Conclusion

- Why do soft skills matter?
- How do soft skills apply to teachers?
- Why do soft skills matter to parents?
- What are the next steps in teaching soft skills to children?

## WHY DO SOFT SKILLS MATTER?

*Soft Skills for Children* was written as a guide for teachers and parents who want to help their children be prepared for the world of challenges, adversity, and problems they may face. However, it was also written to prepare students for the successes, accomplishments, and feats that they will encounter as well. Soft skills are about creating children who are well-rounded, prepared, and ready for the future ahead of them.

Soft skills are skills that will prepare young children for working together in the family unit. Yes, 2-year-old's will still throw tantrums on occasion, and siblings will still fight. Sorry! This book will not cure all the problems of teachers and parents! However, if a child begins learning soft skills at an early age, they will be more prepared to work with others and live harmoniously in the future.

Soft skills will help school-age children learn how to work more productively in school and will prepare them for skills such as organization and time management, which will help in college and vocational schools that will prepare them for future educational endeavors. Applying soft skills to an educational setting will allow parents and teachers to work together to teach students to be college and career ready.

Soft skills will prepare children for the world of future employment. As more and more employers are looking for applicants who are team players, have a positive attitude, and display integrity in their everyday work lives, soft skills will help prepare children for these qualifications as they apply to the work world as well.

*Communication skills* will help children be able to interact with others, share new ideas, and communicate feelings and concerns. They will teach children that listening to others and being aware of body language and non-verbal cues are also ways that kids and adults communicate in the real world.

*Teamwork* will help students learn how to work with others in a kind way and to develop the skills necessary for the world of their future careers. By learning how to collaborate and cooperate, children will be more successful in sports, clubs, and other activities that prepare them for the future.

*Manners* help children learn kindness, compassion, and the skills needed to work with others. Children who have good manners show others that they are caring and kind people who know the social norms to be successful.

Like manners, *respect* is also an important skill for preparing children for the future. Children who are respectful of their peers and the adults in their lives will become workers who are admired and respected in the work world.

*Empathy* helps children learn how others feel and how they can help those who are experiencing problems or need some assistance. The skill of empathy allows children to see how their actions impact others and how feelings can help them in the future.

*Composure,* or maintaining control of one's emotions and anger, will help children be successful both in school and the workplace. By learning how to maintain composure, children will be able to work through the tough times and be able to problem-solve ways to do so later in life.

*Responsibility* is important as it teaches children to do their part in both home and school settings. By learning responsibility as children, they will be able to take this with them into a future career as a great job skill.

*Motivation* is the drive to complete what one started and continue on—even though the road may be rough. Learning to be motivated will help in preparing children to be college and career ready.

*Resilience* is the idea of making it through the tough times and being able to continue, even amid problems and concerns in one's life. Teaching children the soft skill of resilience instructs them an invaluable tool to help them overcome obstacles in their future.

*Integrity* is the idea of doing what is right, even when no one is watching. Integrity is a skill that classrooms need and future employers want in the workers of tomorrow.

*Organization* is important so that children know where their shoes are in the morning and their keys are as adults. However, it is also a skill that will help children benefit more from their education and be more prepared for the workplace.

Like organization, *time management* is also a needed skill for the success of children. Learning to make the most of one's time, use time wisely, and be able to follow plans and schedules are all needed in future education settings and jobs.

*Balance* is also important as it keeps children in check and less stressed. People who can learn the soft skill of balance are able to complete school and work activities while still having time for fun and relaxation.

Finally, a *positive attitude* will take one far in the success of work and school. Children who learn a positive attitude at an early age are those who will continue to use this skill in the future. People who have a positive attitude are not only fun to be around but are appreciated by co-workers and employers.

Overall, the soft skills in this book can be taught by teachers and parents beginning at a very early age. By taking the time and effort to teach these skills, adults show children that they care about their well-being and want them to be successful.

## HOW SOFT SKILLS APPLY TO TEACHERS

Teachers can model and use soft skills in the classroom. By teaching children to communicate, be a team player, and learn organization strategies, they can engage students in a variety of activities that will enhance these skills in the classroom. Teachers play a huge role in making sure that children are prepared and ready for the future they will encounter. They are responsible not just for the content of books, but also in making sure that the children they teach are good citizens and kind people.

Educators are role models for the children in their classrooms. They are being watched by children on a daily basis, and their behaviors and attitudes, whether good or bad, are copied by the children they encounter. By being compassionate and approachable, teachers can let children know they care about their well-being as well as their preparedness for the future. They can make sure that children feel respected and learn responsibility and that they know how to remain composed in rough times.

Teachers can also communicate with parents and families when a child is experiencing difficulty with peers or struggling with schoolwork. They can help form a plan for helping a child be successful and can help locate resources that are needed to assist a child. Teachers can also listen to parents when the children are feeling overwhelmed or experiencing too much homework. Teachers are important as they can help children in many ways beyond simply learning the school curriculum.

In conclusion, teachers play an important part in the development of soft skills in children. By using the teachable moments and spontaneous lessons that occur during the day, teachers can emphasize the soft skills as outlined in this book. Educators are busy people too. They have lesson plans to write, materials to prepare, and meetings to attend. However, realizing that taking a moment to listen to children, helping them learn a new soft skill, and giving them the tools to prepare them for the future is time well spent.

## HOW SOFT SKILLS APPLY TO PARENTS

As stated in the previous chapters, parents play an important role in the development of soft skills in children. Parents are there from the start. They are a child's first teacher, a child's first role model, and the most consistent part of a child's well-being. Parents are there to nurture the scraped knees, the broken hearts, and the hurt feelings. They are also there to celebrate the milestones such as a child's first steps, losing a first tooth, and getting one's driver's license.

Parents start the foundation of a child's life and provide the support, security, and guidance that are necessary to raise a child who has integrity and resilience. Parents can teach manners to children, guide them through learning teamwork, and help them develop empathy toward others. They can also work with other adults such as coaches and teachers to help a struggling child be more successful.

Families are important in teaching soft skills to help children achieve their goals and dreams and to prepare them for success in the school years and beyond. By having a supportive, caring, and safe home environment, children will see how others use soft skills and will be able to take these soft skills into their own futures.

Overall, parents have a huge responsibility to teach children to be well-rounded, caring, and compassionate adults. Only by modeling proper behaviors, providing support, and encouraging students to be their best will this happen. Parents are important people, yet they are also busy people. Working on these skills a bit each day and taking advantage of *teachable moments* can not only help parents deal with the problems that children encounter but also teach about dealing with successes in a humble and kind manner. By learning soft skills at an early age, children will be prepared with competencies needed to be successful at home and in life.

## THE FUTURE OF SOFT SKILLS AND CHILDREN

The world is constantly changing. New technology is created every day, and new skills and aptitudes are needed to help people be successful in their education and careers. Parents and teachers will need to be aware of the constantly changing needs of the world and be ready to learn and adapt curriculum and home skills to meet these ever-changing needs in children. However, some skills will be needed for any child, in any educational setting, and in any career choice.

Soft skills are the skills that will help children learn to be good people, work appropriately with others, and be prepared for future jobs. They are simple to teach and model and do not have to be taught in any certain order. Instead, they are taught as they are needed. When a child has a problem with a friend, then teach about teamwork and respect. When a student loses his homework or can't find assignments, then teach the skills of organization and time management. When a child is feeling overwhelmed, teaching the soft skills of composure and resilience can be helpful.

Being aware of the needs and concerns of the children in our lives, and forming appropriate relationships with them is the best way to start. Parents who know the behaviors and actions of their children, as well as teachers who understand the needs and interests of their students, will be able to assist children when a problem evolves. By knowing about the children in our lives, all adults can use soft skills to help them be better individuals and successful adults.

Soft skills are only the beginning of helping children learn to be the best people they can be. However, by having adults who are kind, nurturing, and caring, children will be more resilient and aware of the problems of the future.

Thanks to the many teachers and parents who will read this book and realize the importance of their role in the development of soft skills in children. The world is hard enough, but by learning soft skills now, children will be equipped with the necessary tools to help them be successful adults and future citizens.

# Bibliography

Ajmera, Ripa. 2019. "How to Teach Children to Have Positive Attitudes." Accessed April 15, 2019. https://www.livestrong.com/article/77539-teach-children-positive-attitudes/ .

Arora, Mahak. 2018. "Communication Skills for Kids: Importance and Activities to Improve." Accessed August 25, 2018. https://parenting.firstcry.com/articles/communication-skills-for-kids-importance-and-activities-to-improve/ .

Bacher, Renée. 2019. "6 Ways to Motivate your Kids." *Parents Magazine*. Accessed April 20, 2019. https://www.parents.com/kids/development/behavioral/6-ways-to-motivate-your-kids/ .

Breaux, Annette. 2019. "Classroom Management Essential: Maintain Your Composure at All Times." *Education World*. Accessed April 10, 2019. https://www.educationworld.com/a_curr/maintain-composure-classroom-management.shtml .

Buscaglia, Leo. No date. "[Loving yourself quote]." Accessed April 8, 2019. https://www.goodreads.com/quotes/299651-to-love-others-you-must-first-love-yourself .

Cambridge Dictionary. 2019. "Definition of Self-Respect." Accessed April 8, 2019. https://dictionary.cambridge.org/us/dictionary/english/self-respect .

Dictionary.com. 2018. "Definition of Soft Skills." Accessed August 6, 2018. https://www.dictionary.com/browse/soft-skills?s=t) .

Dictionary.com. 2019. "Definition of Resiliency." Accessed April 2, 2019. https://www.dictionary.com/browse/resiliency?s=t.

Education Week Research Center. 2016. *Mindset in the Classroom: A National Study of K-12 Teachers*. Bethesda, MD: Education Week.

Elkind, David. 1981. *The Hurried Child*. Boston: DeCapo Press.

Gallegos, Nina. 2019 "Encouraging a Positive Attitude by Creating a Positive Environment." Center for Parenting Education. Assessed April 15, 2019. https://centerforparentingeducation.org/library-of-articles/focus-parents/encouraging-positive-attitude-creating-positive-environment/.

Gopalan, Valarmathie, et al. 2017. *A Review of the Motivation Theories in Learning: The 2nd International Conference on Applied Science and Technology 2017 (ICAST'17)*. AIP Conf. Proc. 1891, 020043-1–020043-7. Accessed April 5, 2019. https://doi.org/10.1063/1.5005376 .

Goldstein, Sam, and Brooks, Robert (Eds). 2014. *Handbook of Resilience in Children*. New York: Springer Publishing Company.

Harvard Health. 2015. "The Importance of Recess." Accessed March 27, 2019. https://www.health.harvard.edu/exercise-and-fitness/the-importance-of-recess .

Indiana Senate Bill 297. 2018. "Employability Skills Curriculum. 2018." Indiana General Assembly. Assessed August 20, 2018. http://iga.in.gov/legislative/2018/bills/senate/297 .

Kennedy-Moore, Eileen. 2014. "Time Management for Kids: Learning about Time Helps Kids Plan, Prioritize, and Work Productively ." Accessed April 12, 2019. https://www.psychologytoday.com/us/blog/growing-friendships/201403/time-management-kids .

Kutner, Lawrence. 2018. "How Children Develop Empathy." Accessed August 5, 2018. https://psychcentral.com/lib/how-children-develop-empathy/ .

Lewis, C. S. (no date). "[Quote about Integrity]." Accessed April 5, 2019. https://www.goalcast.com/2018/03/26/15-c-s-lewis-quotes/c-s-lewis-quote1/ .

McQuerrey, Lisa. 2018. "Why is Teamwork Important in the Classroom?" Accessed August 6, 2018. https://work.chron.com/teamwork-important-classroom-18281.html .

Mehrabian, Albert. 1980. *Silent Messages: Implicit Communication of Emotions and Attitudes.* 2nd Edition. Belmont, CA: Wadsworth Publishing.

Monster.com. 2018. "Soft Skills You Need." Accessed August 6, 2018. https://www.monster.com/career-advice/article/soft-skills-you-need.

Morin, Amanda. 2019. "4 Ways Kids Use Organization Skills to Learn." Accessed April 12, 2019. https://www.understood.org/en/learning-attention-issues/child-learning-disabilities/executive-functioning-issues/4-ways-kids-use-organization-skills-to-learn .

Myers, Pam. 2019. "The Importance of Teaching Manners to Kids." Accessed March 25, 2019. https://childdevelopmentinfo.com/parenting/the-importance-of-teaching-manners-to-kids/ .

National Education Association (NEA). 2019. "Research Spotlight on Homework: NEA Reviews of the Research on Best Practices in Education." Accessed April 14, 2019. http://www.nea.org/tools/16938.htm .

Nemko, Marty. 2018. "Composure: Staying Calm but Focused is an Underdiscussed Key to Career and Personal Success." Accessed April 2, 2019. https://www.psychologytoday.com/us/blog/how-do-life/201807/composure.

Nicholson, Pam. 2019. "Staying Calm During the Storm." Accessed April 10, 2019. https://centerforparentingeducation.org/library-of-articles/anger-and-violence/staying-calm-storm/ .

Oxford Dictionary. 2019. "Definition of Balance." Accessed April 21, 2019. https://www.dictionary.com/browse/balance?s=t .

Price-Mitchell, Marilyn. 2015. "Integrity in the Classroom: How K-12 Teachers Influence Tomorrow's Ethical Leaders." Accessed April 9, 2019. https://www.psychologytoday.com/intl/experts/marilyn-price-mitchell-phd.

Proud to be Primary. 2019. "Teaching Responsibility in the Classroom: An Important Task." Accessed April 19, 2019. https://proudtobeprimary.com/teaching-responsibility-in-the-classroom/ .

Quotabulary. 2018. "Encouraging Quotes for Kids to Shape Their Young Minds." Accessed February 1, 2019. https://quotabulary.com/encouraging-quotes-for-kids.

Spruce.com. 2019. "10 Most Important Benefits of Good Manners in Life." Accessed March 25, 2019. https://www.thespruce.com/how-you-benefit-from-proper-etiquette-1216688 .

Stauffenger, Len. 2019. "4 Steps to a Balanced Life for your Kids: Using a Sandwich." Accessed April 19, 2019. http://www.streetdirectory.com/travel_guide/201606/kids_and_teens/4_steps_to_a_balanced_life_for_your_kids_using_a_sandwich.html .

Talking Tree Books.com. 2019. "Definition of Respect for Kids." Accessed April 8, 2019. https://talkingtreebooks.com/definition/what-is-respect.html .

Teach.com. 2019. "Motivating Students." Accessed April 3, 2019. https://teach.com/ what/teachers-change-lives/motivating-students / .

UNICEF. 2019. "What are Brain Breaks for Kids?" Accessed March 29, 2019. https:// unicefkidpower.org/brain-breaks-for-kids/ .

Van Burean, Abigail. (No Date). "[Quote about responsibility]." Accessed April 14, 2019. http://www.quotegarden.com/responsibility.html.

# About the Author

**Nancy Armstrong Melser** is a mother, teacher, and author. Her first book, *Teaching Soft Skills in a Hard World: Skills for Beginning Teachers*, was published in 2018.

Nancy started her career as a first- and third-grade teacher as well as a gifted and talented educator. She is a professor at Ball State University, where she has taught for 27 years. Nancy enjoys working with students in field experiences, student teachers, and those who have newly entered the teaching profession.

Nancy received her BA in Elementary Education from Indiana State University and her MAE and EdD in Elementary Education and Educational Psychology from Ball State University. She grew up in a family of teachers and is dedicated to preparing students with real-life applications. She has an 18-year-old son, Tyler, who is about to begin his own education in the teaching field.

It is through Nancy's experiences as a teacher, mother, and mentor that she writes this book about soft skills for children.